Handbook for Third World Journalists

Edited by

Albert L. Hester

Wai Lan J. To

The Center
for
International Mass Communication
Training and Research

Henry W. Grady School of Journalism and
Mass Communication
The University of Georgia, Athens

Copyright © 1987   The Center for International Mass Communication Training and Research, Henry W. Grady School of Journalism and Mass Communication, The University of Georgia, Athens, Georgia, 30602, U.S.A.

Note to Users
We encourage use and adaptation of this book in journalism training programs and journalism courses throughout the world. We ask that credit be given to the publication if you make use of portions of its contents. Additional copies of the Handbook are available at cost. For further information, please write to Dr. Al Hester, Henry W. Grady School of Journalism and Mass Communication, The University of Georgia, Athens, Georgia, 30602, U.S.A.

Library of Congress Cataloging-in-Publication Data

Handbook for Third World journalists.

Bibliography: p.
1. Journalism--Developing countries. 2. Journalism--Political aspects--Developing countries. 3. Reporters and reporting--Developing countries. I. Hester, Albert L., 1932- . II. To, Wai Lan J., 1950- . III. Center for International Mass Communication Training and Research (Henry W. Grady School of Journalism and Mass Communication)
PN5648.H36 1987   070   87-71207
ISBN 0-943089-00-X (pbk.)

Acknowledgements

We wish to express our gratitude to the many news reporters, editors, news agency personnel and journalism educators and others who have helped to make this Handbook possible.

We especially wish to thank the following: Dr. Ridha Najar, director of the Centre Africain de Perfectionnement des Journalistes et des Communicateurs, Tunis, Tunisia; Mr. Bechir Toual, Chairman of the Coordinating Committee of the Pool of Non-aligned Countries News Agencies and TAP; Mr. Mohamed Riza, Tunis Afrique Press; Professeur Moncef Chenoufi, Directeur de l'Institut de Presse et des Sciences de l'Information, Tunis; Professor Mehdi Jendoubi, IPSI, Tunis; Dean J. Thomas Russell of the Henry W. Grady School of Journalism and Mass Communication; Bonnie Iwuoha of the Nigeria Union of Journalists; and several anonymous journalists and officials who shared their experience with us, but who could not be identified for a number of reasons.

We also wish to thank R. Ellsworth Miller of the U.S. Information Service, Riyadh, Saudi Arabia; and Ms. Jane Alden, U.S. Information Agency, Washington, D.C., for their early encouragement to make this book possible.

Dedication

Wherever journalists gather, they talk about their jobs. For the most part, they are caring people — people who want to fulfill a useful social mission, people who take pride in their craft of using words and pictures to inform the people in their countries.

I have known enough journalists from throughout the developed and developing worlds to have some feeling for their dedication. I have known Guatemalan journalists who have seen many of their fellow reporters and editors killed in terroristic attacks. I have known journalists in the Caribbean or Asia who must work two or three jobs in order to support themselves and their families.

When these journalists gather, they talk about the problems they face. This book has grown out of their own requests for a special book for Third World journalists, a book which looks their problems squarely in the eye and come up with helpful information which they can use in the face of obstacles they encounter each day.

This book is dedicated to the thousands of reporters and editors who labor for little monetary reward in scores of Third World countries, sometimes in physical danger or sometimes in danger of being overwhelmed by the fatigue of dealing with unresponsive bureaucracies or organizations. May they keep their idealism to present the truth to their societies as they see it, despite the many obstacles and disappointments they often face.

— Al Hester, Athens, Georgia, U.S.A., May 1987.

Contents

	Introduction	1
1	The Role of the Third World Journalists By Al Hester	5
2	Problems of Third World Reporting By Al Hester	13
3	News Values of Three Worlds By Jack Lule	23
4	Understanding International News Flow By Jim Richstad	47
5	Revolutionary and Developmental Journalism By Al Hester	57
6	The Need To Say It Simply By Al Hester	67
7	Covering Especially Tough Stories By Al Hester	75
8	Investigative Reporting: Subjects and Methods By Al Hester	85
9	Environmental Reporting By Mahmoud Abdel Aziz	95
10	Coverage of the Role of Women in the Third World By Edith Nkwazema and "Fatima"	101

11	Beyond Reporting *By Wai Lan J. To*	*111*
12	An Overview of Editing *By Warren K. Agee*	*125*
13	Broadcast News Writing *By Vernon A. Stone*	*135*
14	Putting the Newscast Together *By Vernon A. Stone*	*161*
15	Broadcasting: Serving the Needs of Rural Areas in the Third World *By Al Hester*	*183*
16	Government-Press Relations in the Third World *By An Anonymous Information Ministry Officer*	*197*
17	Education and Training for Third World Journalists *By Al Hester*	*205*
	Appendix I **How to Find News**	*215*
	Appendix II **List of Helpful Readings**	*219*

Introduction

You are a reporter, and this book is for you. Either you have reached a goal you set for yourself of becoming a writer, or someone has asked or even ordered that you be a reporter. We follow different paths to arrive at that place where we become reporters. Our titles are different — perhaps we are termed staff writers, "stringers," correspondents, newscasters — but our goal is the same. We are the latest in a long line of those persons who have been destined to recount events — to recreate today on paper, or over the airwaves, what occurs in the world around them. To report is to tell what is happening, what has happened or what will happen. To be a reporter is to be a teller of stories, the stories of the wonderfully rich and diverse experience of human life, wherever it may be lived.

If you remember one thing in your work, remember that you are the teller of the story of life. You deal with the elemental things which are important to men and women — or you should. You give information which they most need to get along in their daily existence. You let them know what other persons in their community and nation are doing. You recount to them what goes on between them and the people in positions of governmental, business, and educational leadership. The message you bring is often the glue which holds society together.

This wonderful story of recounting, amplifying and interpreting human existence has been told in many forms: the dancers of Tonga who use body movement, music, words and rhythm to link the community together; the drummers of Africa who can convey a vast array of meanings across distance without electronic devices; the printed page, where tiny symbols recreate ideas and help people gain understanding.

You are akin to the ancient travelers who brought the "tidings" or the news from other towns or other countries. How eagerly awaited was the ship which came to an isolated island, perhaps once per year. News was not something to be bored with, to be saturated with, but was something ardently

1

expected and hoped for, then devoured and then digested at leisure. Only persons who have lived in isolated areas or who live where censorship is thorough, can understand the hunger for information, the need to know. To wish to know what goes on, to desire to be tied to the rest of humankind, to seek information to educate ourselves, to make a better life for ourselves and for our children — these seem to be universal human characteristics.

Our societies look to the reporter to bring them information and sometimes entertainment — information to let us cope with life more efficiently, and entertainment to heal our hurts and to make us forget for a moment the difficulties of living. The story-teller has been frequently welcomed, from the days of town-criers who verbally brought important messages to the citizenry, to the appearance of the television journalist who can weave a tapestry of life combining words and sight and sound. You have the capacity of making people think, of making them laugh and of making them weep. But sometimes the messages you bear to them will be so painful that they cannot stand to think about what you tell them, and they will vent their hostility upon you.

At other times you will be subjected to conflicting orders, to being required to put a certain interpretation on your story you try to tell. Your role is so important that neither the power structures of government nor commerce can leave you completely alone to tell things just the way you see them. Often it will be necessary for you to recount the tale of your society in ways which you might not have chosen had you been completely free to present reality as you see it.

If you are fortunate, you will work in a country which allows you considerable freedom to tell the truth as you see it, to give as accurate a recounting or interpretation of processes and events of society as you know how. But even if you are given great freedom by those you work for, you still must deal with those censors or distorters residing in your own mind which require you to paint your portrait of life in certain ways and with certain colors. It is valuable to remember that the external constraints upon transmission of accurate information are just part of the story — your own internal

Introduction

value system, biases, cultural conditioning and philosophy of existence are integral parts of you as a reporter.

As Paul Watzlawick in his book, *How Real Is Real?*, has warned, "the most dangerous delusion of all is that there is only one reality. What there are, in fact, are many different versions of reality, some of which are contradictory, but all of which are the results of communication and not reflections of eternal, objective truths."

The experienced reporter may laugh at this, thinking that "facts are facts," but what is one person's fact is another's fiction. And even when we think of such elemental "facts" as that fire will always burn us, we should also remember that fire-walkers in the South Pacific tread across beds of hot coals with ease, denying our reality with one of their own which is quite different.

The reporter's job is to recount as accurately as possible the shared realities of his or her society or culture.

Reporting, like politics, is the art of the possible. The complete idealist will end up beating his or her head against the rock hard wall of real-life. Experienced reporters learn that is sometimes better to settle for a half-loaf, rather than to strive for the unattainable full loaf of self-expression and freedom to write as they please. Reporters do not function in isolation. They form part of the transmission belt which carries information to the different parts of society. One of the hardest things young reporters have to learn is that at least to some extent they must tell their stories by the rules of those in power.

Whether they write for a major elite daily newspaper in London or a weekly government newsletter in Guyana, they will learn that there is a line which they cannot cross in telling a story which is too unacceptable to their bosses, their nations or communities.

Social controls constantly help shape what the reporter writes. Our political systems, our spiritual beliefs and our interpretations of what reality is all help us shape the tales we tell. Often these tales deal with hard facts, but they also may serve to perpetuate certain feelings and striving in society. The reporter is sometimes the conveyor of myth as well as specific, everyday factual information. When we say "myth" we mean not something false but something so ingrained and so ancient that we do not enunciate it plainly but by subconscious actions and obliquely by how we set the agenda of public discourse and discussion. The way a reporter tells his or her story reflects an outlook about reality and what existence is. For example, many Western reporters have been schooled in the belief that humankind is perfectable, that if we only apply ourselves we can overcome any obstacle to have a fuller and richer life. But some reporters come from societies where obstacles to a good life, are overwhelming, where people die at the average age of 37 rather than 67, where malnutrition is rampant or where a few repress the many. They unconsciously have accepted the idea that life is not perfectable, that we have only quite limited abilities to shape our destinies. And other reporters may see this life as only a wink in the eye of eternity, and realize that the games humans apply themselves so diligently to are soon over and make small difference in the long turn of existence of humankind or of the universe.

So the reporter is counseled to have patience, to have understanding that he or she has one of the most difficult jobs in society, buffeted by political systems, by the desire of private enterprise to make as large a profit as possible, and even sometimes unhonored by those to whom the stories are told. Paradoxically, modern society frequently does not reward the writer or the reporter well, either with money or with prestige. In older times, the story-teller probably had more status than now.

But the reporter is an essential link in the chain of communication which binds people together — or which can drive them apart. To try to fulfill this function in society seems to this writer to be one of the most interesting things to do in life. Our raw materials are men and women and children and everything else in our universe. It is up to us to try to make sense of what is often a fragmented and difficult puzzle to put together. It is our hope that this book can make this important task a bit easier for you.

Chapter 1
The Role of the Third World Journalist
By Al Hester

Is there any reason to write a book specifically aimed at reporters or writers in the "Third World?" Or is there even a "Third World," or is it one of those convenient categories we use to throw things into for the sake of classification?

It is this writer's feeling, backed by much time spent with Third World journalists that there IS a definite need for a book which tries to deal with specific situations and problems faced by many of these reporters and other journalists. And this writer believes, too, that there is utility in grouping together certain countries of the world under the heading of the Third World. Third World journalists themselves have said that they have special needs. If they have received journalistic training, they frequently have used texts aimed at training U.S. or European journalists. The examples in these texts are usually examples taken from American situations, or assuming that the political system is that of the United States.

As Don Woolford wrote recently in the *Australian Journalism Review*, the texts generally on the market from America or Europe are not very suitable for use elsewhere, although they are frequently used because of a lack of anything else.[1] He writes:

"Most English-language journalism texts — especially those of the practical-how-to-do-it variety — come from the United States. They are written for the large American market, use American terms and are firmly set in the American social context. Many teachers from developing countries regard them, at best, as largely irrelevant. A few consider them potentially dangerous. Paul Ansah of Ghana said: 'Young students may accept some of the ideals (in foreign texts) as models without adapting them to local conditions.' Yet, despite these serious reservations, the books are widely used...."[2]

Handbook for Third World Journalists

It is our hope that this book will offer some differing approaches which discuss the role of the Third World journalist and the special situations which he or she frequently encounters. The main difference in the role of the Third World reporter is that she or he writes for and about a nation or society which is at, or near, the beginning of its development as a sovereign entity. The Third World reporter deals every day with a world in flux. He or she cannot automatically assume, for example, that there will be consistency in the outlook of political leaders, that his or her pay check will buy about the same amount of food each week (because of inflation), or that the power will always be on to run the presses in the newspaper or for transmission from the broadcasting station.

The Third World reporter cannot assume even as much as his or her colleague in America or Europe or in a few other highly developed nations that the basics of existence will be taken care of in an orderly manner. Since he or she lives in a world which is changing every day, the Third World reporter must be more alert, more sensitive to what goes on in his or her area or nation.

The reporter from the developed world makes some automatic assumptions which are sometimes wrong, but often correct: that his or her readers will have enough education to understand what is written in the newspaper — or that the reader will have enough money to subscribe to a newspaper. These things are not true everywhere. The Third World reporter must constantly keep in mind that quite a few readers will be newly literate, or they may be persons changing lifestyles from rural to urban.

And the Third World reporter, just as other media professionals in developing countries, can never forget that the media are educators as well as bringers of information to an already educated public. People the world over look to their media to show them models for aspiring to a better life.

When persons need to adapt to new situations, they frequently seek more information to help them, whether it be how to act with correct etiquette in a West African city, or whether it is learning the latest song and dance steps in a Latin American town. It is at this point that the Third World citizens

Chapter 1

frequently absorb information from foreign media. Sometimes they model themselves upon behaviors reflected in the foreign media — behaviors which may or may not be typical of the foreign society, but which have little application to the Third World situation. The Third World reporter has a job to do in educating persons who read his paper as to realities of living in a specific society and culture. This does not necessarily mean a rejection of all outside influences or cultures. But it does at least mean that the journalist will offer something lively and relevant to his or her readers, and it will be generated from the Third World environment.

This writer believes that as reporters learn their craft better in Third World countries, they will be better able to hold their readers and to write stories which will interest them more than the articles about the love-life of a Western movie star.

The reporter in a newly independent and developing society has an even more responsible role than does her or his colleagues in older, more developed nations. If you work as a reporter for the one daily in the entire country, for example, the weight of responsibility is greater than if you are in a country where readers have many papers from which to choose. And there are dozens of Third World nations which still have only one daily newspaper, or perhaps only a weekly publication.

Reporters writing in countries where literacy is low have a heavier responsibility, since those who DO read the paper are likely to be leaders and opinion-makers. If your paper is the only one in your country and it reaches only 5,000 readers, don't think that you do not have an important role: those 5,000 readers have an importance much greater than their numbers suggest.

When we speak of the role of Third World reporters, we should also rememeber that they are pioneers — that they often are the first generation of reporters who are beginning to free themselves from domination by foreign colonial powers. Throughout the Third World, the media were generally set up to serve the needs of the colonial powers, rather than the needs of the majority of the people in the country. Sometimes these needs coincided, but frequently the media concentrated upon the Europeans in the higher social strata or in

7

government, and paid little attention to the other inhabitants. Today, this situation has changed in most Third World countries. The emphasis is away from a press serving mainly the grafted-on culture. The Third World reporter is a leader in changing the perspective of readers. Often, the Third World reporter has the task of holding up the mirror so that his community and nation can see themselves with their new identities forming.

Third World Role Models

Third World reporters can serve, too, as role models for younger persons. It is important that young men and women can see journalists, doctors, teachers and other professionals skillfully at work and not depending upon outside foreign leadership to do the job. A newspaper produced by, and for, Third World people is tangible evidence of independence from outside influences. Even if it is not so skillfully published, or even when its efforts sometimes falter, the newspaper created by Third World journalists is uniquely theirs. The Third World reporter has a major role in such an independent creation in which he or she and the readers can rejoice as their own.

The Third World reporter has another role, a role which Western reporters don't think too much about, although they sometimes practice it, too. This role is to help to convey feedback to persons who make decisions affecting the community or nation.

As Jean d'Arcy has pointed out, much of 20th Century mass communication is "...unilateral, vertical flow of non-diversified information....If we give it thought, we must realize that mass communication is simply the unilateral distribution of information. It is not real communication. Communication implies interactivity." [3]

This statement, when translated, means that consumers of the mass media have been mainly pictured as passive, receiving information from the media but not passing any information back to other sections of society. The Third World reporter should understand that one of his jobs is to focus on situations which reflect the status of people in the community and upon their needs, hopes and fears. By writing about these things, the Third World reporter brings them to the attention of other citizens and political leaders. Not only does the Third World reporter convey information to his readers, he also carries feedback up to the leadership of the community or nation. We hope that the leadership will have ears to hear what the accurate reporter brings back from his work among citizens. Thus, the Third World reporter is concerned, not only with sending information DOWN the line of communication to the media user, but also with carrying feedback UP to those in decision-making jobs. In addition to the vertical flow of communication thus outlined, the reporter should be conscious that much communication should take place HORIZONTALLY, with citizens exchanging information of use to them about what their fellow citizens and neighbors are doing. For example, if one city has found a way to cope successfully with problems of an inadequate water supply, this may be of use to other communities.

So far, we have hinted that there are special tasks for Third World journalists and important roles that they play. These tasks and roles are intimately related to the concept of what constitutes a Third World country. It has become popular in some circles lately to say that the term "Third World" is not very meaningful, that it is inaccurate, since there are so many diversities among nations in Asia, Middle East, Africa, Latin America and the Pacific which carry that designation. What, for instance, does an oil-rich country on the Arabian Gulf have in common with Haiti in the Caribbean, which has one of the lowest per capita incomes in the world? At first glance, we may feel that lumping so many different countries together in only one category is simplistic and does a disservice. But the term "Third World" does still have utility.

The former Egyptian Minister of Planning, Ismail-Sabri Abdalla, has written one of the most telling arguments concerning the concept of the Third World. He traces the historical development of the concept and writes: "It simply designates all nations that did not become, during the historical process of the establishment of the present World Order, industrialized and wealthy." [4] He goes on to remark that "The historical view of the state of our planet is essential for the right understanding of what is the Third World, because it is in the final analysis the periphery of the system produced by the expansion of world capitalism, while the group of European socialist countries is a product of a split in the Centre of the system." [5]

He concludes, "One can safely state that the dependence is with all its corollaries the basic common denominator of Third World countries and comprehensive decolonization is the only path out of it." [6]

Obviously one of the tasks of the Third World reporter becomes the recounting of his country's efforts to change this dependent relationship and to become truly sovereign.

Another less obvious role of the Third World reporter can be to challenge the assumption that "development" is always in the footsteps of Europe or America. By an intelligent, critical questioning of development processes, the reporter in a Third World setting can show that mimicking European or American development may be dangerous. A European, Ignacy Sachs, has pointed out this danger. He is director of the Sorbonne's International Centre for Research on Environment and Development. He wrote in 1979:

"In Northern countries we must start by recognizing our own crisis of maldevelopment. Our attitude is somewhat schizophrenic. At home, we discuss our crisis of structural unemployment, alienation, environmental disruption and inflation. When we come to an international forum, it is taken for granted that what has been happening in the North is good. The only question is by what means the South could reach the same impasse, which does not make much sense." [7]

The Third World reporter will bring intelligent questioning to developmental processes based upon socialist or communist imported models as well. If the Chinese communists can themselves question whether the philosophies and instructions from Marx and Lenin always apply to the Chinese situation at the current time, then it seems wise to make no assumptions that socialist development models should be accepted uncritically. This questioning by the Chinese of blindly accepting communist doctrine and its application to present-day China is certainly one of the most interesting developments of recent years.

Chapter 1

Finally the Third World reporter has a role to play in better informing the developed nations about the Third World. While this may be a secondary role, subordinate to informing his own nation's readers, the Third World reporter can be helpful in presenting a balanced and realistic picture of life in his country. Much of the reporting by foreign journalists about the Third World is derivative — based upon what has already been written or broadcast in a given Third World country. As Third World journalists become more independent and less likely to mimick patterns of coverage used by foreign journalists, this may diversify coverage given to the Third World by the non-Third World media.

If the European countries and the United States media can receive more diversified and meaningful information about the Third World, this could be very important. It could even be argued that a lack of information about Third World realities helps to involve the United States or Europe in various ill-fated military campaigns and adventures in the Third World. Public opinion can be important in the United States in the eventual shaping of foreign policy. Accurate images of the Third World may decrease the chance that ill-thought-out foreign policies will be put into action involving the Third World and the United States and Europe.

Then, too, Third World reporters have a role to play in transmitting news and information to their brothers and sisters in other Third World nations. Those who go through the development process as new nations can frequently lessen the difficulty of development for others by sharing their successes and failures.

FOOTNOTES

1   "Third World Journalism Training," 6:1 (January, 1984), p.66.
2   Ibid.
3   "The 'Right to Communicate' and the Meaning of Words," *Intermedia*, 11:2 (March, 1983), p. 9.
4   "Heterogeneity and Differentiation — The End for the Third World?" *Development Dialogue*, 1978:2, p. 10.
5   Ibid.
6   Ibid., p. 18.
7   "Controlling Technology for Development," *Development Dialogue*, 1979:1, p. 24.

Chapter 2
Problems of Third World Reporting
By Al Hester

In many ways, the problems faced by Third World reporters are like the problems with which a young man or woman just beginning a life of their own must cope. Both the Third World reporter and the young adult are for the first time freed of the dominance of the influence of colonial powers on the one hand, or the parents on the other. This influence can be seen as both malign and benign, but nevertheless the domination has often thwarted the development of the Third World journalist or the development of the adolescent entering upon adulthood.

The Third World journalist or the young adult faces many similar problems, and this chapter will be devoted to an outline of some of them. Every reporter who reads this book will be able to identify with some of these problems and will, no doubt, have others of his or her own to add to the list.

It is only as we dig into what stands in our way of achieving our goals that we can begin a systematic program of getting to where we want to go. Then we are better able to fashion training and to proceed toward more effective work.

The Third World journalist is above all concerned with telling the story of the life of his or her nation or community, as accurately as possible. The reporter is motivated by the desire to transmit and to interpret information in such a way that individual citizens will benefit.

Behind this desire to transmit and interpret needed information is the idea that the mass media serve to hold a community or society together — to give information upon which citizens can base informed judgements, and to facilitate the development of the community or society. Of course, where a commercial press exists, the paramount goal is to make a profit for the owners of the newspaper or other medium of communication. This goal may or may not be compatible with some of the other purposes of having a mass media system.

Not to be overlooked in the outlook the Third World reporter has about his or her work is the desire for personal satisfaction in a meaningful job. Work is important to most of us. We spend much of our time in work activities. If we cannot get personal satisfaction from our jobs and feel that what we do has meaning, life becomes drab indeed. Quite a few of the problems facing Third World reporters impinge upon the reporter's own personal job satisfaction and have to be considered, too.

A young Third World reporter shared with this writer some of his problems as he began his work, after having completed college at his national university. He will not be named, because he is too self-conscious. It was only after the reporter felt he could trust this writer that he gave this intimate picture of how he felt as he went to work on his first job with a national news agency in a Middle Eastern country.

This new reporter found that although he was paid a living wage, there was little incentive to do good work. "Since we all as college graduates had guaranteed jobs, some of my colleagues just came to work to read the paper, to drink coffee and to talk. They frequently didn't even bother to come in. If you really wanted to write, there weren't many examples of people who cared. They were cynical and didn't feel that what they did made any difference," he said.

The Need for Preparation

The young reporter found himself in a rather surrealistic atmosphere, going through the motions of reporting and transmitting the news, but without understanding the background or meaning in his work. While his case is not typical of all, or most, Third World journalists, it does point up the problem shared by Third World reporters and young adults just going out on their own: They must make their own way with little preparation or experience and discover for themselves satisfactions in life, even in the face of depressing circumstances. There is a happy postscript to the case of the young reporter quoted. He received mid-career training of

Chapter 2

more practical nature and was able to rise in his profession to a point where he could influence the way the agency was run, and is a happier person than he was the first unsettling days of his working career.

The problems of adequate training and education will be discussed in more detail later in this book, but it must be said here that one of the greatest problems facing Third World reporters is a lack of much realistic training in school before they go on the job. And meaningful internships or cadetships are still fairly rare in many Third World countries. There are some reasons for the frequent lack of quality in the education of Third World reporters. Many times, their program of study is one which is mainly just talk, where the instructor lectures and discusses theoretical issues, rather than down-to-earth questions.

At many Third World universities, the instructors themselves are academics trained in an academic career, and not overly concerned with making a living in the real work world outside the university campus. Or they hold two or three different jobs themselves, teaching only a few hours a day in a desultory manner. And it must be faced — quite a few educated-class persons in the Third World believe that they should not be involved in anything too "practical," since that has little status. One only has to observe the thousands of lawyers turned out by Third World universities, or the great number of doctors — lawyers and doctors who will probably never practice their professions because there are too many in their fields already — if they stay in the comfortable capital city of their country.

Another more insidious reason for poor preparation for becoming a reporter in the Third World is that for many years, university students could only talk — and talk and talk. Under the colonial systems inherited by the newly independent nations, most of the college students could not look forward to anything but low-level positions. If you cannot influence the political or economic system, you spend a lot of time talking — at least until the time comes when frustration is so great that violence, terrorism, or revolution breaks out. Some Third World students also hate to leave the sheltered world of the academic campus where they have become "professional students," staying on and on in an endless round of make-believe, talking, talking and not doing. But added to the basic inexperience of the new Third World reporter are even more difficult problems which affect his work every day. Perhaps the most basic of these problems is that in a newly emerged country, the entire society is beset by problems. A journalist doesn't do his or her work in isolation — it's done as a part of what goes on in the community or nation. New nations often have few resources, in training, communication, health care, education or in stability in which orderly work can be done.

"You know, my country reminds me of an ant-hill someone has just kicked. The ants are all running around, trying to put things back together, trying to protect the young, trying to fend off the invaders and so forth. We are like that. When we became independent, everything was upset; it was just like the completely mixed-up mess of a kicked ant-hill," one young African reporter told this writer.

A Lack of Money

A lack of money is a major stumbling block that most Third World reporters must face — a lack of personal income for themselves, and a lack of enough financial support for their newspaper or other medium. Often salaries paid to Third World reporters are not enough for them to support themselves and their families. This is true, not only of commercial media, but frequently of government jobs. Tight budgets force wages to be so low that they frequently cannot keep up with inflation, a frequent problem in Third World countries.

The Third World reporter resorts to taking other jobs to make ends meet. In the Dominican Republic several years ago, this writer met many reporters who worked one or two other jobs — going home after working a total of as much as 16 or 18 hours per day. The physical or psychological cost is so high that some reporters feel chained to an endless wheel of existence in which fatigue and "burn-out" are the rule.

This lack of an adequate reporting salary gives rise to another problem — one of taking bribes or "retainers" from

Chapter 2

powerful persons to ensure that they get favorable press treatment when a reporter writes a story. It is all very easy for adequately paid persons to condemn the endemic bribe-taking in many portions of the globe. But what may be abhorrent to the reporter becomes a necessity if he or she is to put food on the table for the family, or to buy a new pair of shoes when the old ones have holes in them. In a number of Latin American countries, many reporters and editors receive a regular "fee" or "retainer" from political leaders or administrators who want a friendly press. Corruption is a way of life in some countries, not only for reporters but for other employees. Everyone understands that to get something done, you have to pay extra for it.

The problem of inadequate salaries is also akin to another economic problem — subsidized operation of the media in many Third World countries. Even many commercial newspapers receive such subsidies outright or in the form of political or government advertising. Some papers have such a slender economic base that they couldn't exist without these subsidies. In some countries, political parties also pay part of the cost of putting out a newspaper. Of course, loyalty to the political party is demanded when this is done.

Those who put out government newspapers are also constantly aware that their budgets may be cut, or they may be dismissed if they displease their governmental superiors.

A Lack of Credibility

Third World reporters also face a problem in credibility. Even if they are ethical journalists, hoping to write accurate accounts of what goes on, public officials and citizens may see the reporter as lacking in education and experience, prone to taking bribes or "selling out to the highest bidder." The problem of media credibility becomes a problem of personal credibility for the individual reporter. If no one has faith in the truthfulness or balance of the publication, then no one will have trust in the reporter who works for that medium.

You can see that almost all of the problems are interrelated. They are all part of a "package" of difficulties the Third World reporter must deal with. This is also true of colleagues in the developed portions of the world, but frequently the Third World reporter's problems are much more acute.

In some nations or communities, political or other leaders use the power of the press selfishly and for their own glorification. If the press of a given community or country has such a reputation, the reporter working for it will have difficulties in credibility and acceptance by the persons with whom he deals and with the readers of the newspaper.

The Third World reporter, while new and inexperienced, and working in a newly emerged nation, must frequently pay the price of a wretched inheritance from previous colonial days. It is a truism that colonies were not set up mainly for the benefit of the native inhabitants. They were established for some tangible benefit of the colonizers — usually economic but sometimes for strategic defense purposes or for reasons of national pride.

These inherited problems are not some political science textbook thing to the Thirld World reporter. She or he must accept the colonial inheritance as reality and deal with it. Although numerous Third World leaders were able to utilize the mass media to establish national parties and to help achieve independence, the press in general before the last few years in most Third World countries was basically there to serve colonial interests. The consumer of the newspaper was mainly the educated colonial foreigner or those working for the governing country and having identical interests. News and information agendas were set to further goals of the colonial government or of outside economic or political powers. Thus usually what press there was developed primarily in the language of the overlords and in the capital city or other major administrative centers.

Telephones, teletypes, roads, railroads and waterways were generally developed to serve the needs of the colonizers. For instance, paths through the jungles in the Solomon Islands were sometimes made by the colonizers in order for them to make tax collections easier among the villages. Little thought was given to whether the paths would serve the needs of the inhabitants. In some cases, this occurred, but in others, the paths linked villages which had been feuding for years and

Chapter 2

made reciprocal attacks easier.
 Often, the transportation and communication infrastructure of the colony developed to extract more efficiently goods and products from agricultural, forest or mining areas. Such development was often lopsided and neglected many portions of a given area, simply because they had little importance to those removing the resources from the colony.
 One researcher, Gerardo Ojeda Castañeda, has called attention to the construction of railroads in Africa for military reasons and for pacification of various areas, as well as for moving the products from plantations and mines to the coasts.

Problems of "Over-Development"

The infra-structure of the typical Third World country often makes communication easier between the country and the capital of the former colonial power than it does among areas in the Third World country. Journalists must constantly deal with difficulties in communication because of sparse telephone and telegraph service, as well as a lack of good roads, frequent rail or air service within their countries.
 Another inherited characteristic is the "over-development" of only the capital city, or a handful of metropolitan areas within a typical Third World country. This great development in one small area, as contrasted to the predominating lack of development in outlying areas, makes the job of the Third World reporter more difficult. The overcentralization of activity in the capital or the few major cities put great stress there and at the same time ignores what goes on in provincial towns and rural areas. The communications media are frequently fairly well developed in the few cities and woefully underdeveloped outside these centers.
 The Third World reporter is tempted, as are other professionals, to flock to the major city and remain there, rather than to be of service in other areas of the nation. In some Third World capitals, there are many newspapers, often small in size, vying for the literate population there, while only anemic and scarce media are to be found in the smaller towns. In some countries an "over-competition" results among media in the capital, while news and information

19

service is lacking outside the central city. Third World reporters must guard against an almost unconscious bias which they may have which tells them that all action is in the capital, and that nothing worthwhile transpires in other parts of the country. If they are not careful, this bias may be reflected in the way they write their stories and how they cover events.

Along with a communication and economic infrastructure inherited from colonial days, the Third World reporter must frequently also use the dominant foreign language of the former colonizers. Many newspapers are published in English, French, Spanish and Portuguese because these were the languages of the persons in power, or of the persons who desired to share the fruits of colonial power. Although not much research has been done, it appears that the forced use of a foreign language creates its own ways of thinking not expressive of the native, original culture of a Third World country. In effect, journalists and others became immersed in the foreign culture and confused it with their own.

Of course, in Third World nations with many different languages, the language of the colonial power did give some linking language understood by considerable numbers of persons throughout the area. This did not make its use more palatable, however, to those forced to use it as a second tongue.

And this brings up another problem: the existence of scores of languages in the country of the Third World reporter. This fragmentation of languages always must make the journalist realize that he or she writes for a more limited audience, or must have work translated into other languages.

Even where readers may understand the language in which the Third World reporter writes, they may not be literate. The reporter always has to be conscious that he or she will not reach many of those who would desire to know what is being said. The printed word may be relayed to illiterates by others in village coffee house or other gathering-places, but its circulation is much more limited than the word over the airwaves, via radio or television.

Chapter 2

The Difficulty of Simplicity

All journalists are told to keep their writing easy to understand. But the Third World reporter must be even more conscious that many readers will have difficulty with anything other than the simplest prose. Third World reporters should always be conscious that it is frequently more difficult to write simply than it is to clothe ideas in complicated terms and jargons. There is also the temptation to write for one's colleagues and news sources, since appreciation from them means a lot. The mass of the readership is nearly voiceless, and praise or condemnation will likely come from only a small group of professionals or decision-makers. Writing to please them is a beguiling thing for all journalists, but especially for Third World journalists.

By this time, the reader may feel that problems are so many and so grave that the Third World reporter would be better off in some other line of work. And it is true that reporting is not for everyone, in whatever country. Reporting is exacting work, but for those who feel there is a need to inform the public about matters of great interest and importance, the rewards can overcome the difficulties. To be a part of the march of history, to help in the "awakening of the slumbering powers within the people" can be one of the most satisfying callings we can have.

Journalists in United States or Europe may have a little trouble in relating to working in the formation of a new nation. But it is well for them to remember that along with their brothers and sisters in developing countries they once also were a part of revolutionary times. Gandhi, Nkrumah, Kenyatta... these have been recent journalists who have helped shape Third World nations. But such journalists as Samuel Adams, John Locke and Tom Paine have all been present at the birth of new societies, too.

A Papuan Statue

Chapter 3
News Values of Three Worlds
By Jack Lule

To many journalists, trying to define news may seem an academic occupation, suitable for tweeded university types. Some journalists may paraphrase Gertrude Stein: News is news is news. Others perhaps liken the news to hunger: They might not be able to define it but they know it when they feel it.

But recent controversies are stimulating appetites for more detailed discussions of news values and proving the inadequacy of "gut-level" definitions of news.

For example, Third World countries express dissatisfaction not only with the quantity of First World news coverage of their nations but also with the values underlying the news. The Third World wants different news values. The Second World offers its own versions but these are unacceptable to the First and may not apply to the Third. Anyone watching such contortions immediately understands: Some definition of news values is required.

Besides global issues of information flow, defining news values packs great personal importance for journalists. From proposals for long-term investigative assignments to live, on-the-scene reports, journalists daily must decide what is news. To only feel and react to news deprives the journalist of insights that might be used to develop new story ideas or angles.

In an economic sense also, the definition of news values is important for journalists. With limited resources, broadcast air time and newspaper column inches, what subjects are selected as news for the day? What subjects are worthy of the journalist's time and attention?

For a practical study of today's concerns, news values manageably can be categorized into the accepted political and economic slots of a First, Second and Third World. The

23

hazards of generalization are great, especially about a subject such as news which allows great distinctions not only among countries but among varied media in the same country. Yet the three-world model does allow a broad discussion of news value distinctions.

This chapter will analyze and compare news values in the First, Second and Third Worlds. It will be shown that the current dramatic difference in world news values is not a recent occurrence but a function of political, economic and philosophical developments of the past three centuries.

First World news values were formed by 17th Century entrepreneurs and continue to be driven by economic factors. Such elements were almost nonexistent, indeed repugnant, in the Second World, where another set of philosophical and economic factors formed different news values. And as the Third World began to break free from colonial domination, news values became even more diverse. With fettered pasts, with fragile futures, Third World nations established their own press systems with values appropriate to their own lands and people.

By chapter-end, journalists may find it more fruitful to paraphrase Shakespeare than Stein by affirming that: News is in the eye of the beholder.

First World News Values

Background: In the beginning was the word, imprinted on the page by the marvelous creation of Johann Gutenberg. Movable type and soon the printing press revolutionized Europe in the 15th Century and gave birth to true mass communication.[1] Indeed, the word "press" still is used to refer to all the media of mass communications.

After the invention of the press, only a small entreprenurial step was required for it to be employed for something called "news". Information, of course, have been passed between people and peoples since the origin of man. But the press made mass dissemination of information a real and profitable possibility. Businessmen found that people would pay for news and by the 16th Century, newspaper

Chapter 3

prototypes — corantos, zeitungs and gazettes — were being published and sold throughout Europe. But what kind of information? What was news then? Surviving samples support the theorists who believe in universal news values because the content of many early newspapers bears remarkable similarities to present-day news content. Al Hester notes, "[A]s we look through the examples of newspaper prototypes from the early centuries of printing, we cannot help but see that the subject matter included much of what is still considered to be 'news' in the West: The doings of prominent persons, the conduct of war, the sensational and the bizarre." [2]

Some early papers recognized and recorded momentous events of their era. In 1493, a broadsheet published a letter from navigator Christopher Columbus who was "purporting to have discovered a previously unknown land." [3] Some papers seemed even to strive to be like today's newspapers of record with all the news that could fit; a German newspaper, published in 1609, was entitled, "Relation of what has happened in Germany and Italy, Spain, the Netherlands, England, France, Hungary, Austria, Sweden, Poland and in all the provinces, in East and West Indies, etc." [4]

Authoritarian control of the press, with restricted content, was accepted through the 17th Century. Newssheets were subject to strict censorship by the era's rulers, such as the Tudors in England, the Bourbons in France and the Hapsburgs in Spain.

But the 18th Century was a time of revolution and new emphasis was given to religious freedom, political rights, free trade and individual liberties, such as free expression. The era also saw the growing emergence of rationalism and scientific thought. More value was placed on the unadorned fact. Objective information was prized.

In the 19th Century, the philosophical aspects of objectivity were aided by economic aspects. With the creation of news agencies and other cooperative news-gathering efforts, objectivity was essential. Agency clients held varying political and religious beliefs. News slanted for one client might offend another. And so objective wire-service news accounts became an economic necessity.

It would be difficult to overestimate the importance of the news agencies to First World news. Indeed, Hachten says, "The history of today's international system of news distribution is essentially the story of the world news agencies and their utilization of progressive technological innovations." [5]

In 1835, Charles Havas was sending financial news by carrier pigion. By 1851, a Havas employee, Paul Julius Reuter had established a telegraph cable link in London. In 1848, the New York Associated Press was begun and in 1907 the United Press Association was competing. "As the telegraph, cable, teletype, wireless (later radio), and communication satellites became operational," Hachten says, "the news agencies or 'wire services' (as they were once called) employed each new device to transmit news ever more quickly from capital to capital." [6]

With the entire world as a beat, with the ability to have live broadcasts from anywhere on earth and then the moon, with the mandate and necessity to fill newspaper columns, use broadcast time and sell information, the great abilities of the First World news agencies has had a direct, and not uncontroversial, impact on news values.

News values: A number of studies and essays have been devoted to the subject of First World news values. Galtang and Ruge, [7] Rubin, [8] and Hester and Eberhard, [9] have compiled their own listing of news values. Such sources, and others, differ slightly in their ranking of news values but there is general agreement on a number of concepts.

TIMELINESS. In the first world, news is now. News is new. News is recent, ongoing and often a continuation of the day or the moment before. In the Hester and Eberhard study of the most commonly mentioned elements of newsworthiness in 25 Western journalism textbooks, timeliness led the list with 84 percent of the texts listing this factor. [10]

"Something new, out of the ordinary, immediate," says Rubin. "Another way to put it, and an important distinction, is the priority on information which is timely, necessary for current adjustment."[11]

Chapter 3

No question that First World media have the ability to provide immediate coverage of news events 24-hours-a-day. The question is why. Why this stress on news on the hour, up to the minute? Some say information can be an edge in modern times. In a fast moving society to be out of date is to be out of the picture.

But psychological factors also might be behind this predominant news value. News, literally something new, gives a sense of change and momentum. Waking in the morning to the news of the past night may give one the inescapable and somehow comforting notion that life indeed does go on.

PROXIMITY. In the First World, news is near. Readers want to read about their continent, country, state, county, town, neighborhood, street or, most preferably, their next-door neighbor.

Diamond says the U.S. news media have responded with firm equations of proximity: "10,000 deaths in Nepal equals 100 deaths in Wales equals 10 deaths in West Virginia equals one death next door." [12]

PERSONALITY. News is prominent people, public persons. Throughout the First World, politicians, royalty, sports heroes and heroines, movie stars, the famous and infamous hog the headlines. Some are so prominent that their every move is news. A president's vacation or a pregnant princess' dip at the beach becomes page-one news.

"Personality creates news," Rubin says. [13] He quotes Howard K. Smith, former television anchorman: "Television news is pictures, plus word, plus personality." [14] Of course, this news value of personality is so strong that television anchormen become personalities in the news.

Jeremy Tunstall has found a certain structure to the media's portrayal of personalities. "News values are explicitly hierarchical — people at the top of governments, organizations, trade unions, or football teams are assumed to have more interesting things to say, and thus receive more attention than do mere voters, employees, union members or reserve players."[15]

Besides having interesting things to say, public persons may be news worthy for other, less tangible reasons. The public might be living vicariously through the exploits and escapades of its public personalities. Thousands of trees have given their lives [for newsprint] to provide news coverage of Elizabeth Taylor marriages. Thus is the power of the personality news value.

UNUSUAL EVENTS. News is weird. News is bizarre. Odd occurrences are news in the First World. The value is passed on to journalists through the most hoary of news cliches: If a dog bites a man, there is no news, but if a man bites a dog, there is front-page material.

This news value, perhaps more than any other, has been subject to sharp criticism. James Reston has concisely stated the problem. He says, "We are fascinated by events but not by the things that cause the events."[16]

Although the value is easy to criticize, strong tides pull on the reader and the journalist, causing them to focus on unusual news events. Way back in 1922, Walter Lippmann was recognizing and identifying these forces: "The point is that before a series of events become news they have usually to make themselves noticeable in some more or less overt act. Generally too, in a crudely overt act." [17] And Lippmann offered explanations for such a news value. His thoughts are eloquent enough to quote in full:

"The news is an account of the overt phases that are interesting, and the pressure on the newspaper to adhere to this routine comes from many sides. It comes from the economy of noting only the stereotyped phase of situation. It comes from the difficulty of finding journalists who can see what they have not learned to see. It comes from the almost unavoidable difficulty of finding sufficient space in which even the best journalist can make plausible an unconventional view. It comes from the economic necessity of interesting the reader quickly, and the economic risk involved in not interesting him at all, or of offending him by unexpected news insufficiently or clumsily described."[18]

HUMAN INTEREST. News is ordinary people, their peculiarities, similarities, huge kindnesses, petty meannesses — all the glory and shame of the human spirit can be news in the First World.

Chapter 3

Two New York City stories can serve as examples of this news value. In 1984, a New York detective finished a meal at his regular restaurant and told the waitress that instead of giving her a tip he would fill out a state lottery ticket with her and split any winnings. The ticket proved to be the big winner and, true to his word, the detective split millions of dollars with the waitress. The story was headline news in New York for a week.

At year-end 1984, on a New York subway train, a man shot four youths, criticallly injuring one, who had asked him for money. For weeks, the story raged, with citizens and journalists debating whether the man was an heroic vigilante or a law-breaking assailant. The only sure answer was that the event contained remarkable news value.

Once again, Lippmann offers reasons for the newsworthiness of such stories. He says a reader wants a "sense of personal identification with the stories he is reading. News which does not offer this opportunity to introduce oneself into the struggle which it depicts cannot appeal to a wide audience. The audience must participate in the news, much as it participates in the drama, by personal identification." [19]

CONFLICT. In the First World, news is fights and disagreements. In city council meetings or Parliament, on the streets or the battlefields, if people are fighting, there's good chance it is news.

As the First World found in the 1960s, riots and wars endure as news. Otis Pike, a *Newsday* columnist, writes, "If it isn't awful, it isn't news.... There has to be some middle ground between Pollyanna and the Angel of Death, but the news media can't seem to accept good news as news." [20]

Some say that the news media's preoccupation with conflict is only a reflection of human fascination with the same. And human fascination with conflict may simply be a vicarious thrill and emotional outlet for the news public.

Reporting First World news values: An important element in a discussion of news values is how those values are handled in individual stories. Many processes take place between the journalist's decision about the news value of a story, the writing of that story and its appearance in a newspaper or newscast. The presentation of news values in the news is the function of this short section.

"While news values are crucial in the paradigmatic SELECTION of events, they play only a part in the syntagmatic CONSTRUCTION of those events into stories," says John Hartley in his book, *Understanding News*. [21] Hartley says four basic assumptions underlie the journalist's transformation of news values into convenient categories not-so-coincidentally conforming to the sections of a Sunday newspaper, such as politics, international affairs, sports, leisure, etc.; society is composed of individuals who can "make news" and effect change by their actions; society is hierarchical, logically and orderly organized; and society has a "concensual" character that recognizes "our" interests.[22]

With news values in mind, with societal assumptions organizing the material, the journalist then is free to apply STYLE to his construction of the story. Objectivity, of course, is the hallmark style of First World news. We have seen how news objectivity was developed centuries ago by wire services in response to varied clients' demand for nonslanted information. Although as we shall see in the following section, analytical and interpretative reporting continue to gain favor, objectivity still is the stylistic key to First World news.

Signs of Change. First World news is changing. Its values, structures and styles have been affected by changing readership, the demands of increasingly complex societies and the development of alternative press systems in the Second and Third Worlds.

James Reston writes about the modern newspaper but his comments can apply to all First World media: "The modern newspaper is searching for a new role, or should be," he says, "and that role lies in the field of thoughtful explanation.... We are no longer in the transmitting business, but in the education business."[23]

This change is affecting news values and news styles. First World journalists are learning that education sometimes can be accomplished not through the objective reporting of events but through the interpretation and explanation of those events.

There have been calls for other changes in First World news values. Jeremy Tunstall, writing in *The Media in Britain*, says, "Much of what happens in the media is so muddled, so confusing (to audiences, to critics and defenders, as well as to journalists and producers) precisely because in the very same material both INEQUALITY and AMBIGUITY are overtly present — for example in 'news values'." [24] Tunstall gives the BBC as an example. He says, "The BBC enshrines ambiguity in its vague and apparently contradictory traditional goals of education, entertainment and information." [25]

Some U.S. editors have called for the humanization of news values. Michael J. O'Neill, editor of the *New York Daily News*, asks, "Is our duty to inform so stern that we exile ourselves from our humanity?" [26] He answers, "We should begin with an editorial policy that is more positive, more tolerant of the frailties of human institutions and their leaders, more sensitive to the rights of the feeling of individuals — public officials as well as private citizens." [27]

Such thinking seems to be in line with that of the ultimate critic of First World news values: the First World public. A 1984 survey of American newspaper readers commissioned by the American Society of Newspaper Editors, found that "sample readers still complain about a lack of fairness, about sensationalism, manipulation, and emphasis on bad news." [28]

The numbers should be disturbing to First World journalists: 52 percent of sample readers charged newspapers with sensationalizing the news. However, this figure looks good in a comparison: 80 percent charged television with sensationalization.[29]

It is hoped that such surveys, discussions and studies of First World news values will insure that values continue to be defined and refined. David Shaw, media writer for the *Los Angeles Times*, says, "For too many years the press was a powerful institution dedicated to the critical examination of every other powerful institution in society — except itself." [30]

Second World News Values

Background: News in the Second World, for our broad purpose, is defined as that news from within nations aligned with the Soviet bloc. To some, this news is pure, communist party propaganda or government controlled messages that have little to do with concepts of news. To others, this is the first real alternative to a "corrupt" system of First World news.

In the mid-1800s, news in the Second World was developing along the same lines as the First. In Russia, after the censorial reign of Nicholas, mass newspapers thrived in the 1860s.[31] Tabloids blazed with war news and local scandals; other large dailies offered concise, objective accounts of events. Some papers even offered veiled criticism of the government. Similar news was available in Poland, Germany, and other East European countries.

Political revolutions eventually revolutionized news within the Second world. In Russia, the reform movement of the late 1800s had become vocal and strident. Strict censorship was instituted. Yet expatriate, Marxist, and other underground presses continued to flourish. By 1912, the Bolsheviks' *Pravda* was being published in St. Petersburg, despite censorship and harassment.

Revolutionary news values were highly specialized. Stories were labor oriented. Strikes, meetings, mobilizations and labor theory were the steady diet. Workers were used as correspondents. Other workers had long letters printed. Some articles were instructive in heady matters of philosophy or minute matters of organization. These revolutionary papers not only were forming a new government but a new concept of news values.

After the 1917 revolution placed the Bolsheviks in power, *Pravda* was established as the official party organ. The revolutionary concept of news became an institutionalized theory of news.

Aided by the power of the press, Lenin had achieved a revolution. Thus, he was aware and wary of press power. Within three days of taking office, Lenin outlawed opposition newspapers. His reasoning was clear; his expression frank.

Chapter 3

"Why, if a government believes it is doing right, should it allow itself to be criticized? It would not allow opposition by lethal weapons, and ideas are much more fatal than guns." [32]

Thus, in place of the ribald, economically competitive, politicking press of the First world, Lenin put forth perhaps the single most quoted theory of news values: "The press should be not only a collective propagandist and collective organizer but a collective agitator."[33]

An integrral part of Leninist philosophy, this concept of the press thus has been established to some degree in all countries with Marxist-Leninist governments. Though there are marked distinctions among individual press systems in the Second World, the media share this common source and philosophy of news.

News values: Within the media of the Second World, full discussions of news values often take place. As a key element of state legitimacy, the press and its role are thoroughly explored in books, periodicals, broadcasts, editorials and the front page of the party newspapers. From these sources primary characteristics of Second World news values can be ascertained.

IDEOLOGICAL SIGNIFICANCE. News is correct ideology. Certainly this is the overriding factor in determining news in the Second World. Every decision in the news process, from story selection to presentation on the page or the screen, is made with considerations of ideology.

Pravda devotes a number of front-page stories annually to a discussion of the press' role in a socialist society. Hammered home is the importance of ideology. On page one of September 17, 1983, *Pravda* said, "Journalism is rightly called life's reconnaissance worker. The potential of its active participation in molding contemporary man's outlook and life stance and in asserting the moral and spiritual values of the Soviet way of life is today greater than ever.... Ideological commitment and skill — these are the two wings that lift journalism to the level of the demands made on it by our complicated time." [34]

The ideology of course is Marxist-Leninist. But news is not the simple reprinting of dogma. News is the interpretation of the "way of life" in ideological terms. "The deeds and concerns of the life which the party and all Soviet people are living today comprise the main content of our press," *Pravda* said on another occasion.[35] In portraying this life, the newspaper said, journalists should "display a high level of social activeness and responsibility and seek in their activity to be guided by the Leninist principles and traditions of party journalism."[36]

To overestimate the ideological factor in considering Second World news values would be impossible. Indeed, the following elements of newsworthiness can be seen as subheadings beneath the one dominant category of ideological significance.

PARTY CONCERNS. The Communist party is news. What the party says, what the party does, what the party thinks, what the party does not think — this is news in the Second World.

The predominance of the party in Second World life is the reason behind this news value. These are societies where most of life's activities are controlled by the party. So such a news value makes great sense and is of real help to a media public.

Certainly, this news value also aids the party. Legitimacy of authority can be given by such comprehensive coverage. And this value also is of help to journalists whose job positions often are a result of party positions.

This link between party and media is reflected, indeed celebrated, in the Statutes of the Association of Journalists in East Germany: "Being faithful and reliable co-militants of the Party of the working class and the Government, they contribute their convincing gripping, publicistic work reflecting real life to the further growth of the developed socialist society."[37]

SOCIAL RESPONSIBILITY. News is responsible to society in the Second World. News is constructive and positive, active and vigilant. For example, East German journalists are supposed to "contribute by their work to the formation and strengthening of socialist convictions."[38]

But contrary to the views of some in the First World, journalists in Second World do engage, in fact are encouraged to engage, in criticism of wrong-doing. The trick is who, what and how much to criticize. Naturally, state ideology and high party officials are not usually subject to investigation or abuse. But let there be a bureaucratic problem or a low-level official caught with a hand in the till and the media will respond with astonishing scorn.

Pravda gives its blessing to such a news value. "The duty and vocation of the press is to submit to the public's verdict the questions which worry people and to make bold use of criticism in the struggle against impediments to our progress."[39]

EDUCATION. In the Second World, news is instruction. News teaches. News preaches. Inherent to its function as propaganda, Second World news does not exist of itself but for a purpose. That purpose often is education. Unlike in the First World, Second World news is not meant simply to inform or entertain; it may be informative and entertaining but only in the process of education.

The code of ethics of the Czechoslovak Union of Journalists exemplifies this educational emphasis. Article 1 describes the union as a "unified ideological-educational and special-interest voluntary social organization of journalists."[40] Article 2 says the group's task is to "organize and to guide journalists so that they consciously and with initiative contribute to the construction of a developed socialist society, so that they help particularly to educate people in a socialist spirit and contribute to raising the political and cultural maturity of the citizens of a socialist state and to develop their constructive activities."[41]

Such education can take many forms: articles on agricultural innovations; health care tips; televised language instruction; pamphlets and books on Lenin, and ever-present explanations and denunciations of Western imperialist doings. The plentifulness of educational news is a clear indication of its value in the Second World news system.

HUMAN INTEREST. This news value is a close relation to similar values in the First World. News is of, about and for people. But in the Second World, this value typically is given an ideological touch. News is not so much about people as it is about THE people. When Second World news media highlight "ordinary" workers, such as when *Pravda* displays a large photograph of a worker on the front page, this is not meant to elevate or extol a particular person but to elevate all workers.

Letters to the editor are a tremendous, thriving aspect of this emphasis on people in the Second World. They can give people a real or imagined sense of partnership with the media, a desirable display of unity. *Pravda* claims to receive 500,000 letters a year.[42] The use of worker correspondents is another display of the news value given to the interests of the people.

SOME FIRST WORLD VALUES. It would be incorrect to assume that traditional First World news values, such as timeliness, proximity and prominence are absent from Second World news. For example, when Pope John Paul II returned to his homeland of Poland in 1982, the event was treated as a major news story because of news values such as proximity and prominence. The difference between First and Second Worlds, however, is that such news values always would be subservient to primary ideological concepts.

Reporting Second World news values: Presentation of Second World news also is shaped by ideological factors. The same elements that form the basis of news values also affect the structure and style of Second World news.

Thus, the ideological component of a news story is not hidden subtly within the body. Ideology is stressed, examined and interpreted for readers. *Pravda* says, "To know how to dig down to the essence of a phenomenon, to sweep aside tall stories and boastful exaggerations, to champion state interests more boldly, and, at the same time, to describe our system's real achievements and advantages with emotion and passion, to reveal the nature and makeup pf modern people, heroes of the 5-year plan — this is the social imperative for publicists today." [43]

Chapter 3

Second World news is subjective, personal. It attempts to create a sense of passion and commitment. There often is a tone of unity to the news, not unlike the consensual nature of First World news. Press reports often will begin, "The Polish people deplore the actions..." or "The nations of the world rejoice at the prospect...." Editorial and stylistic decisions thus are made consistent with Second World news values.

It might be instructive to note factors absent from Second World news style. News is not objective or sensational, it does not contain many negative events nor does it probe the private lives of its public figures. These concepts, staples of First World news styles, serve no ideological purpose and thus for the Second World, they are not a part of the news.

Signs of change: By their very nature, Second World news value have been resistant to change. Designed to defend, protect and extend the legitimacy of the Communist party, the press is the righteous defender of a revolutionary status quo. Change under such conditions is difficult.

Yet stylistic changes recently have been occurring. They have interesting implications for global news concepts because there are some suggestions that just as First World news is evolving toward more subjective, interpretative reports (hallmarks of Second World news), news in the Second World appears to be evolving toward the use of more factual material and objective accounts. [The recent U.S.S.R. emphasis on "glasnost" or "openness," is being reflected in the socialist world.]

Evidence of this change can be seen in *Pravda* editorials on the role of the press. The newspaper has called for the use of facts and news items to enhance the effectiveness of the press. Press organs "use concrete facts to reveal the indissoluble link between CPSU policy and people's vital interests," *Pravda* said in a 1983 editorial. [44]

On another occasion, the newspaper said, "One of the most important tasks which the party has set Soviet journalists is to be constantly concerned to enhance the effectiveness of items. This is achieved on the basis of specificity, pithiness, immediacy and party passion of the items published." [45]

Rilla Dean Mills studied twelve years of *Zhurnalist*, the official monthly of the Soviet Union of Journalists and concluded that "a move toward more objective reporting seems to be taking place in the minds, if not always the practices of Soviet journalists." [46]

Mills quotes a Soviet managing editor discussing norms of objectivity for professional journalists with an ardor that would do the First World proud. "One of those norms...(is) an absolute impartiality," the editor said. "A lack of preconceptions in his research, which guarantees that he will not take a one-sided approach to people, to events. It is a very strict standard." [47]

Third World News Values

Background: News values of the Third World are broad and varied. The great diversity of Third World countries, from China to Chile to Liberia, guarantees a great variety of news. But common sources and values can be found.

The development of the Third World in modern terms of technology and economics has been relatively recent. Many countries did not begin their struggle against colonialism until the 20th Century. But for centuries before this, there have been full, vital communication systems operating throughout Third World countries.

In India, even before the 10th Century, monks and missionaries moved from village to village with illustrated morality stories and scrolls. What was news then to these pioneer correpondents? "They preached the equality of man and talked of mutual help, love, compassion and truth," says one historian. [48]

In the 8th Century, there were even long-range "op-ed" discussions in India. It is said that Haribhadra of Bhinnamala quickly wrote a rejoinder on a philosophy work by Rajashekhara, who lived a thousand miles away in Magadha.[49]

By the 17th Century, there was an irregular government news service operating in India. The newspapers were small, eight inches by four and one-half inches, and handwritten.

Chapter 3

News then also was small in scope. "The ambit of news coverage, however, was limited: the emperor was the news." [50]

Some of the later Third World newspapers seemed to have news values quite recognizable to the West today. The first papers in Sri Lanka, then Ceylon, "contained (government) notifications, literary and political contributions, descriptions of marriages, obituary articles and even merry quips." [51]

Even some political protest was accepted. *The Liberia Herald*, created in 1826, carried the motto, "Freedom is the Brilliant Gift of Heaven." [52] "Political protest and the expression of informed African opinion soon became the dominant theme of the West African English language press," says Graham Mytton. [53]

In the 20th Century, a common theme united the many diverse cultures of the Third World: development. Under this heading has been grouped a large number of issues, including the removal of political and economic restraints imposed by the First and Second Worlds, the bid to gather benefits from advanced technologies and economies and, not least, the establishment of communication systems more applicable to Third World nations.

Ortega and Romero were writing specifically of Peru but their words can apply to all the Third World when they point out just how strong is the "close relation between the social and economic structure and the use and ownership of the mass media." [54]

News values: Efforts have been made in the Third world to establish sets of news values as alternatives to those of the First and Second World. Although some journalists consider some Third World news proposals threats to press freedoms, issues at least have been raised, questions have been asked and a much needed focus has been given to the discussion of news values. What follows is a listing of current, predominant Third World news values.

DEVELOPMENT. Athough another chapter in this book covers developmental journalism in detail, the concept must be

39

mentioned here. It is a primary news value in the Third World. News is progress. News is growth. News is new dams, new buildings, new roads and new countries.

Much of the final report of UNESCO's 1980 MacBride Commission dealt with the issues of development and journalism: "Communication can be an instrument of power, a revolutionary weapon, a commercial product, or a means of education; it can serve the ends of either liberation or of oppression, of either the growth of the individual personality or of drilling human beings into uniformity. Each society must choose the best way to approach the task facing all of us and to find the means to overcome the material, social and political constraints that impede progress." [55]

SOCIAL RESPONSIBILITY. News is responsible. Although this value probably holds sway throughout all worlds, within the fragile structures of Third World nations, responsible news is considered imperative.

For example, the code of ethics of the Indian Press Council states that "Journalists and newspapers shall endeavor to highlight and promote activities of the state and public which aim at national unity and solidarity, integrity of India, and economic and social progress." [56]

In January 1984, the Conference of Ministers of Information of Non-Aligned Countries was held in Jakarta, Indonesia. One of the "appeals" to come out of the conference was for the world's mass media "to eschew tendentious reporting in all its manifestations and to desist from propagating materials which directly or indirectly may prove detrimental or prejudicial to the interest of any member country of the Non-Aligned Movement." [57]

This is the flip side of positive, developmental journalism. Not only are journalists asked to concentrate on the good, the positive, the building, but they are asked to ignore or downplay the bad, the negative and the failures.

Such an appeal may strike some as a threat to press freedom. Kenyan editor Hilary Ng'weno has an answer. "The challenge to the press in young countries is the challenge of laying down the foundations upon which future freedoms will thrive," he says. "Under some of the conditions in which vast numbers of Asians, Africans, Latin Americans live, it would be sacrilegious to talk about press freedom, for freedom loses meaning when human survival is the only operative principle on which a people lives." [58]

NATIONAL INTEGRATION. This value is the logical extension of developmental and socially responsible journalism. By concentrating on the positive achievements of a nation, news might serve as a stimulus to national pride and unity. For embryonic nations (and for new governments that want to hold on to power), such pride and unity is invaluable.

Speaking of disunity and tribalism still found in countries of Africa, Ng'weno says, "In such countries, the first duty of the press, as indeed of any other institution or individual, is to encourage greater national unity; for without a minimum amount of national unity all other human values in society become impossible. Freedom and justice become meaningless. Life becomes insecure. Where there isn't enough national unity, it is my view that the press should confine itself to the difficult task of helping to unify the nation and removing mistrust between communities or tribes."[59]

This view is not confined to Africa. Hahn Bae-ho has written of Korea, no stranger to disunity, "Inasmuch as the achievement of national integration is an overriding goal of the Republic of Korea, the concept of freedom of the press has to be defined in the context of this objective." [60]

Another Korean scholar, Oh-Inhwan, polled 370 of his country's journalists and found that 90 percent agreed the press should contribute to unification of the nation. [61]

EDUCATION. In the Third World, news teaches. News instructs. News can be used to pass on knowlege of health care, to aid in agricultural work, and to spread cultural works. In rural villages, where one radio might be the sole source of communication with the country at large, such use of the media seems a necessity.

There is another, less obvious aspect to this news value of education. As an educational tool, news can be used to set the agenda of the nation. Mahatma Gandhi expressed this news value. "One of the objects of a newspaper is to

41

understand the popular feeling and give expression to it," he said. "Another is to arouse among the people certain desirable sentiments; the third is fearlessly to expose popular defects. [62]

Indira Gandhi voiced similar thoughts. "If information is power, it is not merely the power to impose, but also the power to resist," she said. "The non-aligned should view communication in this sense. For us it is a major resource in enlarging our people's awareness, and in securing their participation in national and international affairs." [63]

OTHER NEWS VALUES. Although they play secondary roles in the Third World, some news values are quite similar to those found in the First World. According to Matta, recency, proximity and personal interest are "intrinsic qualities" of news in the Third World. [64]

Reporting news in the Third World: As in the First and Second worlds, the presentation of news in the Third World is a function of the primary news values. Construction and style of news stories are consistent with the values of developmental, socially responsible and educational journalism.

Good news is freqquently played up; bad played down if it is mentioned at all. Styles are personal and subjective, not unlike the Second World, attempting to elicit commitment and unity from the news public. The Declaration of Principles of the National Union of Journalists of El Salvador reflects this intense commitment: "The National Union of Journalists of El Salvador is an anti-imperialist, anti-colonialist, popular, and democratic organization, which adopts methods of struggle corresponding to the revolutionary process the Salvadorian people initiated to materialize their objectives." [65]

But there are signs that some journalists in the Third World also recognize the economic value of entertaining, informative news. Dayo Duyile wrote of Nigerian communications, "The chief purpose of social responsibility is to inform, entertain, sell and raise conflict to the plane of discussion. The Nigerian press involves itself in all of these." [66]

Chapter 3

Signs of change: Thus far, change is the only constant in Third World news values. Change within the Third world. Change within individual countries. Generally, it can be said that many Third World countries' press systems bear similarities to those of the Second World. Governments are involved with the news. News is employed in pursuit of national goals. Much of the First World's negative reaction to call for a new world information order is based upon the Third World embrace of such news values.

There are also indications, however, that First World news concepts, such as objectivity, have exerted their influence. A statement issued by the Nicaraguan Journalists' Union in early 1984 said, "The mass media should orient their news toward an analysis of the country's problems from an objective standpoint in conformity with reality." [67]

And in India, Indira Gandhi had complained that "Many of our own journalists consider it smart to imitate the popular Western definition of bad news being good news and are bored by constructive and developmental activity." [68]

Yet perhaps it will be from the Third World that truly universal news values develop. As elements of First and Second World news values move closer, as Third World journalists continue to select from each in creating values of their own, there may appear a common ground among news values. Some differences always will remain because nations always will differ. Yet more similarities may become apparent, similarities that may reveal the universal value of news.

FOOTNOTES

1 For a short discussion of early communication systems, see Robert W. Desmond, *The Information Process: World News Reporting to the Twentieth Century* (Iowa City: University of Iowa Press, 1978), pp. 1-28.

2 From his UNESCO paper, "Synthesis of Western Viewpoints," (Paris: UNESCO, 1980), p. 8.

3 Desmond, p. 21.

4 Heinz-Dietrich Fischer and John C. Merrill, eds. *International and Intercultural Communication* (New York: Hastings House Publishers, 1976), p. xii.
5 In his *The World News Prism* (Ames, Iowa: The Iowa State University Press, 1981), p. 18.
6 Ibid.
7 Johan Galtung and Mari Ruge, "Structuring and Selecting News," in Stanley Cohen and Jock Young, eds. *The Manufacture of News: Deviance, Social Problems and the Mass Media* (London: Constable Publications, 1973), pp. 62-73.
8 Barry Rubin, "International News and the American Media," in Dante B. Fascell, ed. *International News* (London: SAGE Publications, 1979), pp. 181-243.
9 Hester, p. 11.
10 Ibid.
11 Rubin, p. 213.
12 E. Diamond, *The Tin Kazoo* (Cambridge: MIT Press, 1975), p. 94.
13 Rubin, p. 213.
14 Ibid.
15 Jeremy Tunstall, *The Media in Britain* (New York: Columbia University Press, 1983), p. 142.
16 James Reston, *Sketches in the Sand* (New York: Knopf, 1967), p. 195.
17 Walter Lippmann, "The Nature of News," in Charles S. Steinberg, ed. *Mass Media and Communication* (New York: Hastings House Publishers, 1972), p. 143.
18 Ibid., p. 148.
19 Ibid., p. 150.
20 *Newsday*, Long Island, New York, December 30, 1984, p. 9.
21 John Hartley, *Understanding News* (London: Methuen and Company, Ltd., 1982), p. 81.
22 Ibid.
23 Reston, p. 194.
24 Tunstall, p. 153.
25 Ibid.
26 *Wall Street Journal*, May 6, 1982, p. 28
27 Ibid.
28 *Christian Science Monitor*, May 21, 1984, p. 3
29 Ibid.

Chapter 3

30 *Christian Science Monitor*, April 12, 1984, p. 22.
31 James Markham, *Voices of the Red Giants* (Ames, Iowa: The Iowa State University Press, 1967), p. 37. This classic still is a most valuable reference for discussions of Russian and Soviet communications.
32 Ibid., p. 104.
33 As cited by V. Glukhov in "Mass Communication Media in the USSR," *Democratic Journalist*, July-September, 1981, p. 17.
34 *Pravda*, September 17, 1983, p. 1, as translated by the Foreign Broadcast Information Service, Washington D.C., (hereinafter cited as FBIS).
35 *Pravda*, January 27, 1983, p. 1, FBIS.
36 Ibid.
37 Sepp Horlamus, *Mass Media in CMEA Countries* (International Organization of Journalists, 1976), p. 59.
38 Ibid.
39 *Pravda*, January 27, 1983, p. 1, FBIS.
40 Horlamus, p. 27.
41 Ibid.
42 "Some Facts About *Pravda*," *Democratic Journalist*, July-August, 1982, p. 37.
43 *Pravda*, July 2, 1983, p. 1, FBIS.
44 Ibid.
45 *Pravda*, January 27, 1983, p. 1, FBIS.
46 Rilla Dean Mills, "The New Soviet Journalism: More Facts?" *Newspaper Research Journal*, Fall, 1982, p. 28.
47 Ibid., p. 30.
48 M.V. Desai, *Communication Policies in India* (Paris: UNESCO, 1977), p. 14.
49 Ibid.
50 Ibid., p. 22.
51 M.A. de Silva, *Communication Policies in Sri Lanka* (Paris: UNESCO, 1977), p. 23.
52 Graham Mytton, *Mass Communication in Africa* (London: Edward Arnold Publisher Ltd., 1983), p. 38.
53 Ibid.
54 Carlos Ortega and Carlos Romero, *Communication Policies in Peru* (Paris: UNESCO, 1977), p. 19.

55 As cited in Oswald H. Ganley and Gladys D. Ganley, *To Inform or To Control? The New Communications Network* (New Delhi: Hindustan Publishing Corporation, 1982), p. xvii.
56 Desai, p. 32.
57 "Jakarta Appeal to the Mass Media," *Democratic Journalist*, February, 1984, supplement.
58 Mytton, p. 59.
59 Ibid., p. 60.
60 Hahn, Bae-ho, *Communication Policies in the Republic of Korea* (Paris: UNESCO, 1978), p. 14.
61 Ibid., pp. 27-28.
62 Desai, p. 25.
63 Indira Gandhi, "Communication for International Cooperation and Mutual Understanding," *Democratic Journalist*, February, 1984, p. 7.
64 F. R. Matta, "Concept of News in Latin America," *Democratic Journalist*, April, 1979, pp. 4-8.
65 "Declaration of Principles," *Democratic Journalist*, January, 1982, p. 10.
66 Dayo, Duyile, *Media and Mass Communication in Nigeria* (Ibadan, Nigeria: Sketch Publishing Company, 1979), p. 24.
67 "Statement of the Nicaraguan Journalists' Union," *Democratic Journalist*, April, 1984, p. 19.
68 Indira Gandhi, p. 6.

Chapter 4
Understanding International News Flow
By Jim Richstad

The flow of news — its fairness, its balance, its usefulness — has been at the center of the international debate over world communication for more than a decade.

The Non-Aligned Movement in the early 1970s put the issue on the world political agenda by calling for a "new international information order." The Non-Aligned Summit statement on communications in Algiers in 1973, for example, called for reorganization of "existing communication channels which are the legacy of the colonial past, and which have hampered free, direct, and fast communications" among Non-Aligned countries."

The Algiers summit called for Non-Aligned countries to "exchange and disseminate information concerning their mutual achievements in all fields" through the mass media of their countries, and to share experiences in communication with one another.

A related concern to news flow imbalance is the parallel imbalance in communication resources. Richard Butler, secretary-general of the International Telecommunications Union (ITU), makes the point, for example, that in 1982 there were some 550 million telephones, 600 million television receivers, 1.4 million telex terminals and thousands of data networks and other special-purpose transmissions systems, and "90 per cent of these service installations are confined to some 15 per cent of the existing nations, 85 per cent of the nations use the remaining 10 per cent." The United States alone has half of the world's telephones.

The 1974 UNESCO General Conference in Nairobi discussed the news flow issue in the context of the "mass media declaration," and forced the issue center-stage. The "mass media declaration" move forced Western media organizations and governments' attention to the issue of world news flow, and it since has been a major world concern. Participants in the Dag Hammarskjold Third World Journalists' Seminar in New York in 1975 argued that the Third World needed a better flow of news so that people in the developed world would understand better their condition, and support the New International Economic Order (which many countries had called for earlier).

The Third World Journalists' statement said: "True political liberation will continue to be strongly handicapped unless steps are taken to break the hold that news agencies reflecting interests that are not those of the Third World have on the information sent to, or originating in, the Third World countries."

The mid-1970s saw the full emergence of the news flow issue, in the context of the new international information order and the new international economic order. The often fiery debates in UNESCO and other fora, on both Third World and First World sides, generated animosities and bitterness, and charges of "cultural imperialism" and "government control" were almost commonplace at international meetings.

The charges by the Third World and others were clear: the world news system was run by the developed world through the great international news agencies — the Associated Press, United Press International, Reuters and Agence France Presse. The result was, intentional or not, a one-way flow of news from the developed countries to the developing countries, they alleged. And it was a distortion of what little news there was about developing countries, a lack of relevant news for the Third World countries and how they are handling their problems. The world news was presented, they said, everywhere with a Western perspective, seen and reported "through Western eyes" and Western value systems, the Third World critics said.

Deliberate Manipulation?

In broader scope, Non-Aligned spokesmen like Mustapha Masmoudi of Tunisia and American critical scholar Herbert I. Schiller charged that Western news, government, military and business interests were deliberately manipulating

Chapter 4

the flow of world news to their advantage, to keep the Third World in a dependency position. Masmoudi as late as December of 1984 was still attacking the Western news agencies in ungiving terms, despite great advancement to take heat out of the arguments, and despite some compelling empirical evidence that the flow was never as unbalanced, biased or irrelevant as many of the early critics contended. Masmoudi, speaking to a Non-Aligned meeting in New Delhi, said: "We are witnesses to ruthless commercialism combined with permanent cultural aggression, which compromises our economies, undermines our social traditions and alienates our children. The powerful are always right. It is time the voices of the weak were heard."

Western arguments came down hard on many Third World countries for asking for a free and balanced flow of news internationally while effectively restricting the national press and outside journalists. How, Western interests asked, can there be a fair and balanced picture of the Third World when those countries don't allow their own journalists much freedom to report, and when they hamper international journalists from reporting in their countries? There are plenty of cases for the West to point to — jailings, beatings, suppression and obstruction — that illustrate their point.

By 1976 at UNESCO's Nairobi meeting, the issues were clearly drawn, and Western journalists and governments were prepared, for the first time, to meet the Third World arguments head on. For starters, the West adamantly opposed the "mass media declaration," as proposed, as permitting government control of international communication. The compromise that evolved was the establishment of the International Commission for the Study of Communication Problems, or the MacBride Commission, as it was known. The Commission took a world view of communication problems, and did a careful and full inventory of these. The flow of news was a central problem, and was viewed as a serious matter within countries as well as between and among nations.

What was noticeably and painfully lacking from the debates over news flow and international communication was evidence one way or the other, on such charges as "cultural imperialism", "imbalance," "bias," and "distortion" in the news flow. A great deal of anecdotal information was being presented to "prove" cases for or against, and figures were apparently grabbed out of the air or gained from impressionistic reading and viewing of the media. Since the first part of the 1970s, that lack of empirical data on the central news flow questions has dramatically changed. There is now extensive research on the flow of news questions, and the results give a firmer basis for the discussion of the issue.

The Third World's flow of news concerns were well-suited to empirical analysis through the use of content analysis methods, and several major studies were undertaken in the mid-1970s. The results of these studies, reviewed here, show quite a more complex and different pattern of world news flow than the critics pictured earlier. The studies also show the limitations of a strictly quantitative approach to news flow — there needs to be more attention to the actual content of the news stories in a qualitative assessment. But, given the questions raised by the Third World critics, the news flow studies of the late 1970s and early 1980s provide much-needed clarification to the issue.

There are probably by now hundreds of studies of the flow of international news. Most of them, however, are of limited scope, and were not designed primarily to test the issues raised in the new world information and communication order (as UNESCO developed the concept) debates. Others are of the flow from one country to another, or perhaps from several countries to one of particular interest.

Global Information Order

Hamid Mowlana, in reviewing international research at the 1984 International Association for Mass Communication Research (IAMCR) congress in Prague, contended that "because of the tendency to focus on a few actors and factors, and because of a paucity of systematic research, the present state of knowledge in international flow of information is rather fragmented." But, he also noted, "we are in a much better position today to draw a rough skeleton of the global information flow than we were a decade ago."

Chapter 4

Mowlana in his review of international flow of information, said that "more often than not" a directional flow from the North to the South was shown by the research, and that there was a notable lack of "exchange of data, news, information, cultural programs and products, and persons among the developing countries." The research showed an improvement in the quantitative flow of news but that "cultural and ideological distortion and biases have been predominant during the last several years...."

Other points noted in the flow studies include "the growth of technology is not necessarily increasing the access of all peoples to information, nationally or internationally," and that there is an imbalance as well in research on information flows, with underrepresentation from South researchers.

●●●●●●

The review that follows is primarily based on three major efforts of the late 1970s — the Pacific Basin Flow of News Study, which this writer directed with Tony Nnaemeka of Nigeria; the Southeast Asia flow study directed by Wilbur Schramm and L. Ervin Atwood, and the very large "The World of News" project of the International Association for Mass Communication Research (IAMCR) and UNESCO, with many participating researchers from around the world and directed by James Halloran of IAMCR. All three efforts include a wide geographical area with many countries, and all are premised on the issues of the new international information order.

The Pacific Basin study included more than 30 countries and newspapers. A one-week period in late 1976 was studied for news content in newspapers representing the Pacific Islands, Oceania, Asia and North America. Four hypotheses derived from Johan Galtung's work were tested, and the data supported each. The study found a classical pattern of colonial-structured news flow:

●There was a one-way flow of news from the Center countries (Britain, Australia, New Zealand, France, and the United States) to the Pacific Island countries.

●There was a preponderance of Center news in the press of the Periphery countries.

51

- There was little or no news of the Periphery countries in the Center countries' press.
- There was little flow of news between Periphery countries.
- There was even less flow of news between Periphery countries of different colonial-based blocs, such as the American, British and French areas.

There was, however, evidence of a breakdown in the colonially structured pattern because of the introduction of satellite technology and a news exchange conducted over the satellite. There was also evidence that the Pacific Island countries' news attention changed with the coming of independence, and that the countries would find their different places in international flow patterns. Western Samoa, independent since 1962, was associating more and more with other Third World countries, in a news sense, while Fiji (independent in 1970) and Papua New Guinea (independent in 1975) actually increased attention to Center countries after independence.

The study also developed the "news from nowhere" concept that seems common to other studies: the source of international news in the press in developing countries is very often not identified for the reader (in our study, this was the single-highest "source" of international news).

The Schramm-Atwood study of the "Circulation of News in the Third World — A Study of Asia," covered 19 principal dailies of Asia, the four Western international news agencies, and innovatively traced several major news stories and even conducted a readership survey. The results were a comprehensive picture of the flow of news in Southeast Asia, among Third World countries. The two researchers found that Third World countries were getting much more news about other Third World countries in a QUANTITATIVE sense. The researchers also concluded that that did not necessarily mean that the QUALITATIVE flow of news was adequate. That, they said, was for further research.

The study developed the concept of regional news patterns with data showing most of the Third World news in a particular country was about its neighboring countries. Third world news in East Asia newspapers, for example, was about

Chapter 4

East Asia countries, and so on. Later studies have shown this over and over, and it is accepted as one of the tenets of world news flow. Nnaemeka and this writer developed out of the study the concept of "information regions," which relies heavily on geographic regional news flows. Clearly the broadcast-based studies reported through the mid-1980s were organized by the IAMCR as "The World of the News" project. IAMCR, acting at the request of UNESCO, organized 13 research teams from around the world, and the United States team covered 16 additional media systems, making a total of 29 systems from all regions of the world. Newspapers and broadcasting services were included in the study. Data collection was for a chronological week and a "composite" week in 1979. The results summarized here are taken from Annabelle Sreberny-Mohammadi's article in the Winter, 1984, *Journal of Communication* and the U.S. reports from *Foreign News and the New World Information Order*, by Robert L. Stevenson and Donald Lewis Shaw (editors).

The study was designed to answer some of the questions raised in the new world information order debates, and was a relatively simple (methodologically) content analysis, but by its scope of 29 press systems became a complex study.

Study Findings

A key finding given first was that, despite different levels of development and political perspectives, "the overall pattern of attention paid to certain kinds of events was remarkably similar." The study found also that politics — international and domestic — "dominated international news reporting everywhere." The prominence of regionalism in international news coverage also emerged, as it has in many earlier studies. "News by exception" was common everywhere. There was a high rate of non-attribution for news sources, making it difficult to accurately assess the impact of the Western news agencies, a major issue in information order debates.

While news about the immediate region predominated, news from the United States and Western Europe rated second in news attention.

53

Stevenson in a separate article said the study DID NOT "show that Western media and news agencies ignore the "Third World," nor that the Third World was singled out for "unfair negative coverage." He noted also that the Western media DO NOT ignore the Third World, with about one-third of the news in the Western media systems about Third World countries. More than two-thirds of the news in Third World press systems was about Third World countries. On the question of "bad news," Stevenson notes that such news is a small part of the flow — with politics dominating. And on "bias," the studies showed most of the news was "neutral," neither for nor against anything.

Some of the researchers involved in the IAMCR study, such as Kaarle Nordenstreng of Finland, repudiated the study, charging that the "project was dominated by 'vulgar' categories that capture 'ad hoc' aspects of the media content, rather than a comprehensive image carried by the content." Others called for more focus on qualitative aspects of news flow in future research.

Stevenson and Shaw conclude in their book that "many of the issues raised in the world information debate are less problems of Third World journalism than problems of journalism that all practitioners of the craft need to address. All media systems define news narrowly, all reporters quote a narrow range of newsmakers, all editors put a heavy emphasis on what happened today in the world's hot spots."

Problems of Flow

There are, of course, many particular problems that Third World journalists face in trying to present international or any kind of news to their readers and listeners and viewers. These have been well detailed by such early writers in the field as Lloyd Sommerlad, and include many issues that UNESCO and other organizations have been addressing. These include such obvious matters as training of journalists, costs of sending and receiving news report, government restrictions, small market bases for news and mass media products, often difficult circulation problems for the press and limited coverage for broadcast services, old and outdated equipment,

Chapter 4

inadequate repair services, low levels of pay and prestige, lower level of education, translation from English or French into national languages, and probably many others from country to country. These are not small problems, and no matter how much UNESCO, government information services, professional organizations, and international training institutes do, they are not problems that will disappear overnight, and probably not for decades.

There are many obstacles in the Third World to an adequate flow of international news. Several developments over the past decade, however, are promising. Training of Third World journalists is moving ahead on many fronts. Such training is one area, for example, that ideological differences are less important — professional journalists in the West and in the Third World have a way of going to the pragmatic problems of training writers, editors, news directors, camera crews and so on.

Another development that is already improving the flow — at least the technical transmission among countries — is satellite communication. Other technological developments offer similar promise. The possibilities of South-South communication, for example, steer around one of the major obstacles or concerns of the information order — funneling of world news through Western news agencies.

The concurrent growth of national news agencies and exchange agreements is another positive factor in improving the flow of news for Third World countries. The Western agencies, realizing the impossibility of adequately covering the world by themselves, have in recent years cooperated in these developments in important ways.

The recognition of regionalism in news flow as recognized by the studies points to an area where special efforts may produce big improvements in the quality of news available to Third World editors and news directors.

Stronger regional agencies have emerged in the last decade, as an example, and offer new alternatives to Third World countries for international news more suited to their needs.

One development that grew out of the news flow concerns of the mid-1970s, perhaps with much of its promise

55

still unfulfilled, was the establishment of the alternative or complementary news service of the Non-Aligned News Pool. Recently, the Non-Aligned News Pool members have shown a pragmatic interest in improving their report, which has been criticized as not being very high in news interest. The possibly more workable Inter Press Service, the Third World News Agency, offers important alternatives, also.

Another factor recognized in the flow studies is the changing pattern of Western news agencies in regard to Third World news.

As the studies show, there seems to be an increasing amount of Third World news being made available by these news agencies, both to Third World countries and to the Western media.

The obstacles in the flow of news for Third World countries remain large and will take time, effort and resources to tackle. The particular problems, however, are much clearer now than they were a decade or so ago, and national and international efforts can be directed toward such basic problems as training, equipment, national news agencies and news exchanges.

Chapter 5
Revolutionary and Developmental Journalism
By Al Hester

Probably necessary outgrowths of the attempt to free a country from outside domination are the two types of journalism which give this chapter its title. Revolutionary journalism dedicates itself simply and completely to opposing and overthrowing forces which the people of a given society do not want ruling them. Developmental journalism is a natural outgrowth of revolutionary journalism in that it seeks to call into being a nation and to develop it and to carry out the ideals set forth in the earlier revolutionary phase.

Revolutionary and developmental journalism are frightening things to defenders of the status quo. Sometimes such journalism is impassioned, nonobjective and even polemic in nature. Sometimes these kinds of journalism are heir to the serious vices of furthering the careers of selfish leaders and factions. And yet other forms of journalism can be as perverted in the service of false gods, too. Any form of the press without some active sense of social responsibility can be a tool for injury. For instance, critics of the commercial, U.S. press system wonder how publishers can fatten their pocketbooks through the acceptance of advertisements of products unquestionably damaging to the health of millions of persons, such as tobacco products. And yet it has only been through the "watchdog function" of the federal government that any attempt at regulating the advertisement of such products has really been made.

Learning by Mistakes

One of the most difficult things for parents is to let their children test their wings as they grow up, to live the kinds of lives they may desire, or even to make necessary mistakes by which they learn. It is also difficult for former holders of power such as colonial governments to "let go" and to allow their former "children" to pursue their own destinies. Of course their inexperienced protegees will take false steps, fall down, have to pick themselves up and try again and again to reach maturity. The world's history is almost uniform in showing that stable societies must go through periods of strife, disorganization, fearfulness of outsiders and self-centeredness before they can assume their more mature roles. And some nations, just as some children, may never grow up to fit our conceptions of useful and stable members of the world society. Every family has its ne'er-do-well son or daughter, the one who has reprehensible behavior or who just can't seem to "turn out right."

The price of national sovereignty, just as with individual independence, is that some nations as well as individuals will choose to go their own willful way, taking a road we would not have them take. But the alternative is to impress upon them an outside will which will rob them of their individuality and freedom of choice.

Revolutionary Journalism

Most Third World countries have at least gone through the initial stages of rebelling against foreign domination. They may in many cases still have to rebel against leaders who do not have the true national interests at heart, but this struggle becomes a very personal one in which outsiders can scarcely tell which causes are just and which ones are not. It is interesting to note that the United States of America went through a stage of revolutionary journalism which lasted for several decades before and during its own Revolutionary War. Its famous Committees of Correspondence were specifically set up in 1772 as an efficient method of finding out what was going on in the frequently disorganized American colonies, reporting these developments in opposition to the British government and focussing public sentiment against the colonial power. It can be taken as a rule that where ever existing forms of journalism or communication do not serve the needs of informing the people, alternative modes of

Chapter 5

sharing information will spring up. This is true whether we are dealing with 18th Century America or the 20th Century U.S.S.R., with its numerous underground, samizdat, publications.

It is fascinating to review the North American revolutionary process. We could be talking about a 20th Century struggle for independence in Africa as we read the description given to the work of Samuel Adams, one of the most dedicated American Patriot journalists and publishers:

"As a propagandist, Adams was without peer. He understood that to win the inevitable conflict (with Britain), he and his cohorts must achieve five main objectives. They must justify the course they advocated. They must advertise the advantages of victory. They must arouse the masses — the real shock troops — by instilling hatred of enemies. They must neutralize any logical and reasonable arguments proposed by the opposition. And finally, they must phrase all the issues in black and white, so that the purposes might be clear even to the common laborer. Adams was able to do all this, and his principal tool was the colonial newspaper.[1]"

These goals of Adams' revolutionary journalism have remained the goals of more recent attempts to overthrow dominating powers. For instance, in Africa, we could find much similar journalistic practice by Kenyatta, Nkrumah, Kaunda, and others, as they sought to organize opposition to foreign rule and to form national independence parties. As North American journalism scholar Willliam A. Hachten has pointed out, revolutionary journalism feels no loyalty to the government it seeks to overthrow.[2]

And it must be said that so-called "objectivity and fairness" are not very much in evidence in such desperate battles. The historian will look in vain for large quantities of objective reporting in a study of North American revolutionary journalism, even at the founding of a democratic nation. So certainly it is asking quite a bit to expect to find those objective qualities in the revolutionary press of other developing countries.

If you are a journalist who labors in a country still seeking its independence from foreign rulers, you are probably well-acquainted with the strengths and weaknesses of revolutionary journalism. There is another kind of revolutionary journalism which still goes on later in the struggle to achieve just societies. This is a revolutionary journalism which seeks to cause change, overcoming exploitive situations, or which seeks to better the lot of the people of a given nation. Such journalism does more than merely passively report what goes on or just interpret it — it attempts to bring the light of exposure to destructive situations and to help clean them up. Sometimes such journalism is called investigative journalism or reform journalism. A later chapter will discuss many situations in which such journalism is a necessity in the developing world.

Developmental Journalism

It is almost amusing to listen to the hue-and-cry raised by some free press advocates when they consider "developmental journalism." They find it difficult to understand that in nations with scarcely any resources the press must be a means to fleshing out the structure of national independence begun in the revolutionary journalism period. It is logical for leaders of a new nation to ask: What shall we do to BECOME the nation we desire to be? That is what the process of national development is about: trying to overcome the problems inherited from the pre-independence period, to give some form to the cry of ordinary people for a better life. Such critics are either too far removed from their own revolutionary roots or too identified with those who would maintain the status quo regardless of its injustice.

Critics of developmental journalism are really criticizing what can be a perversion of it — its utilization by leaders for attaining selfish goals. There are legitimate criticisms to be made if all dissent is throttled or if every journalist and every citizen must be completely orthodox in his or her beliefs. But there is nothing inherent in developmental journalism which means it must be a more evil form of journalism than journalism driven by the profit motive.

Probably the majority of the journalists in the Third World countries work in a communications field basically dependent upon the national government for its existence. It

Chapter 5

is a fact of life that the aims and policies of the national government will be furthered through the national journalism. Many Western critics make the automatic assumption that governments can never have the welfare of their citizens at heart as much as a "free and independent " press. This writer doesn't think much research has been done to study whether "laissez-faire" press systems have a better record for furthering the public good than have governmental press systems. Of course, strict libertarians will argue that the press is completely apart from trying to achieve good or evil outcome — that it is there merely to report and to call attention to interesting situations. It is the belief of this writer that every press system has its agenda of involvement with society. Only naive persons believe that the press sits in splendid isolation, not furthering causes or utilizing the flow of information to its own advantage. The very selection of stories is in itself non-objective. Our chapter on news perceptions and news values attempts to show that there is little evidence of a mere random chronicling of chance events coming to the attention of the journalist.

The commercial press systems of the world mostly have as their foremost goal making money for their owners. Frequently choice of news stories and display of the news is based upon what will increase street sales of papers. In most news rooms of private enterprise papers, the reporter and editor are at the mercy of management which decides the "news hole" (what is left over after the advertisements are laid-out). If the paper does not turn a good profit, it will go out of business or be sold to someone else. This ceaseless "bottom-line" constraint of making money is the main guiding idea for many private enterprise newspapers. Some are excellent papers despite the pressure — or because of the pressure — to make money. Others, however, show little sense of concern for the public, outside of keeping it pleased enough to buy more and more papers or more and more products advertised in the newspaper.

Most reporters and editors who have worked for private enterprise newspapers also can cite many cases of "trade-outs" of stories to advertisers for purchasing advertising. That is, the advertiser not only gets what he pays

61

for in the ad — he gets a "puff" story pushing his business or product.

This writer frequently had to do business "booster" stories telling what wonderful opportunities that were in special year-end merchandise sales by leading merchants in a large U.S. city. These stories were done, not because they had very much news value, but to stimulate thousands of citizens to spend more money with advertisers.

Media for Modernization

In most Third World countries, the mass media "... are primarily expected to function as parts of the national effort in the gigantic task of modernization," Amde-Michael Habte, has written.[3]

He notes that the Western values of a "free press" often "...take a back seat when freedom from poverty, disease and illiteracy becomes the overriding issue."[4]

If we look at developmental journalism, we see it generally has the following characteristics:

1. The communications system is an integral part of the national government. It often is run through a Ministry of Information or Communication. In many Third World countries, there was no real journalistic infra-structure inherited from colonialist days, or if there was, it did not unite the new nation but linked it to the seats of colonial political or economic power.

2. The journalists of the country, either implicitly or explicitly, are asked to take part in achieving the major tasks of nation-building. These include, but are not limited to, upholding the new political system, helping citizens to understand that the new nation does indeed exist, trying to overcome poverty, starvation, disease, illiteracy and ignorance, and to preserve the cultural heritage of the people.

3. The mass media of the country are often required to follow some sort of outline or national communications policy set by the central government to help obtain national development.

4. The press needs to be "guided" in its efforts to help

Chapter 5

achieve the goals of nationhood. The amount and type of such guidance may vary from heavyhanded, authoritarian, measures such as censorship and intimidation, to leadership which allows many differing approaches to the common goal of national development.
  5. Usually, journalists are government employees.
  6. If private, commercial journalism exists in the country, it is expected to consider the national interest above its own particular, private interest. If it cannot do so, it may not play the needed role in national development.

Developmental journalism, as practiced where the government has a communications monopoly or near-monopoly, can easily lend itself to serious abuses. Where dictatorships exist, the dictator finds it extremely tempting to turn the energies of the press to keeping himself in power. The goals of national development become of little importance where the preservation of her or his personal power is at stake. If the press is integral to government institutions, it can be more easily perverted to such efforts. But to condemn all developmental journalism as the handmaiden of selfish leaders is a narrow view. Is there anything which makes Third World leaders more selfish, more evil, more prone to forget the needs of their people than leaders of the developed world? Western critics of Third World governments frequently are victims of the "we"-"they" categorization of humanity. "We" are always more enlightened, more democratic, more civilized and more ethical than "they".

Is it not possible that at least occasionally, political leaders of Third World countries have the welfare of citizens at heart as much as leaders in Europe or in the United States?

Although journalism-in-the-service-of-national-development may lend itself easily to manipulation and selfish ends, it is still the basic fact of existence for many Third World journalists. It doesn't matter very much to them what outside critics think of the system — it is the system with which they live and of which they are a part, sometimes even be free choice.

Much of the rest of this book will be devoted to ways in which reporters and editors can do a better job within the

63

realistic confines of their jobs. No journalistic system is a Utopia. Even the "free" Western journalist will not bite too severely whatever hand is feeding him or her. But we CAN ask the question: How may I as a reporter or editor improve my skills and my work to serve my goals and that of my community or country?

The Western European democracies and the United States had the luxury of several hundred years in the process of their development. The new nations formed within the past few decades do not have so much time. There are thousands of their citizens dying of starvation, of poor hygiene, or from a lack of skilled nurses and doctors. Millions cannot read words printed on a page. Scores of countries are still mostly dependent upon what other nations will pay for basic raw materials and a few natural products. The national income of developing nations is frequently at the whim of the marketplace buying a single crop or product. The nations carry an increasingly impossible burden of debt to industrialized nations — taking a staggering proportion of the national budget.

Is it any wonder that developmental journalism has come forward as one way to stimulating national development? Is it surprising that the preservation of some form of order and national identity where only chaos existed a few years ago may be high on the agenda of a new nation?

The mass media can be — and are — agents of social change. The people of a given nation are influenced by the saturation of messages coming from their mass media. The bombardment is even unconsciously received by many. Role models appear on television and in films.

This writer remembers very well a survey his Mexican university public opinion survey class students made in the city of Guadalajara a few years ago. Residents were surveyed concerning their movie-going habits and what they got from the pictures they saw. Many said they looked, not to see the plot unfold, but to study the ways of dressing and behaving shown in the movies depicting other lifestyles. There was little doubt about the strong impressions made on these Mexicans, especially by the foreign films. Some even fashioned their own courtship habits by observing men-women relationships in other countries, as depicted on the screen.

Chapter 5

The developmental journalist must have some idea of the vision held for the development of his or her nation. This may come from government communication policies and the journalist's own definition of national development. The story of national development can be exciting, not just the dull reporting of routine events or reporting the doings of a leader with a big ego. Frequently citizens of new nations work against great odds to create a fuller and better life for themselves and those who will come after them. To catch this vision and to expound the dreams of a free and good life is a worthwhile task. The telling of the story of national development does not imply that we must tell a story of just positive achievement.

If you are lucky, you will practice journalism in a country where leaders have the maturity to see that they may make mistakes. Many of the problems faced by the new Third World countries are extremely hard to solve. There may be false starts and wasted effort (this is also true of Western countries). It may be a service to your country for you to be able to point out development programs which are not working. The developmental journalist, just as any other journalist, must frequently ask the question "Why?"

One of the most engrossing stories throughout the world is the battle women (and sympathetic men) are making to improve the position of women in society. The developmental journalist may wish to be an acute observer in telling this story involving betterment for one-half of humanity. Just as journalists have called attention to the evils of racial and class prejudice, so are they calling attention to discrimination against women because they are women.

Efforts to cut down unemployment are also good stories for the development journalist. One of the most demanding situations in many Third World countries is the failure of citizens to find work. They are forced into emigration to richer nations, into criminal activity or sometimes into working for only a pittance or a few hours daily. The development journalist can tell in human terms the loss to human dignity caused by low employment or under-employment, and can focus on possible ways of curing the problem.

65

The developmental journalist cannot forget that he or she is an educator as well as a reporter. The need to learn new information is a crying need in new countries. Stories which point out the effects of drinking contaminated water and how citizens can guard against water-borne diseases may mean the difference between life and death. The educational task is especially necessary where citizens have had not much chance to get a basic education.

The chapter on investigative reporting will go into more detail about some of the ways in which Third World journalists can be active participants in the development of their community or country. Frequently the Third World journalist does not have the luxury of being a mere observer of the scene. In a new country, the journalist cannot divorce himself or herself from the struggle for a better life.

As Dr. Wilbur Schramm, one of the journalists and educators most cognizant of Third World problems, has pointed out, the media can help to create a climate for development. They can alert citizens to dangerous situations. They can focus attention on a need for change. The media can also help to raise the aspirations of a people, and the media can create a sense of nationhood.[5]

FOOTNOTES

1 Edwin Emery and Michael Emery, *The Press and America* (5th ed.) (Englewood Cliffs, N.J., U.S.A.: Prentice-Hall, 1984), p. 69.

2 *The World News Prism: Changing Media, Clashing Ideologies* (Ames, Iowa, U.S.A.: The Iowa State University Press, 1981), p. 70.

3 See his "The Mass Media in the Third World," in *Comparative Mass Media Systems*, by L. John Martin and Anju Grover Chaudhary (New York: Longman, 1983), p. 100.

4 Ibid., p. 109.

5 Dr. Schramm's book, *Mass Media and National Development* (Palo Alto, Calif., U.S.A.: Stanford Univ. Press, 1964), still is one of the best discussions of the role of mass communication and national development. Dr. Schramm does not pretend that the mass media can by themselves develop a country, but he points out graphically how the media have their roles to play in the process. It is a helpful background reading for reporters and editors.

Chapter 6
The Need to Say It Simply
By Al Hester

If readers can't understand what you have written, then why write it? Journalistic writing is writing to give the reader understanding or information he or she didn't have previously. If the reader can't comprehend what is in your news story, then no communication has taken place. Or if the reader gets bored, irritated or puzzled by your story, he or she will most likely go on to something else more interesting.

One important thing to remember: there is no contract signed by your reader which requires him or her to read what you have written. Many writers seem to think that just because they write a story it will be read. A humbling experience is to sit on a bus or in a waiting room at an airport and watch how people read newspapers. They casually glance here and there, for the most part, picking very quickly which stories, pictures and headlines interest them and ignoring the rest. They may not read your story. The writer, editor, news photographer and newsroom artist must all work closely to present as interesting a "package of information" as possible.

We usually find that few readers read more than a half dozen paragraphs of stories in which they have an interest. Perhaps one of every ten readers will read the story from start to finish.

The average time spent reading a U.S. newspaper — and these papers are huge compared to those in much of the rest of the world — is probably only about 15 minutes. In these mammoth papers, hundreds of stories compete with each other for the attention of the reader.

You may write for a publication which has only eight pages, but readers still must be seduced into reading what you have written. Your tools are writing about subjects which interest them and doing it in such a way that it is easy for them to understand and sometimes even entertaining them. And you most often have to do this in only a few hundred words.

In several other chapters of this book we try to help you pick subjects which may be of interest to many readers. Generally they will be interested in things which affect their personal lives. Most of us have trouble relating to abstract things — like the national deficit in millions or billions of pounds, pesos, etc. It is only when we can relate it in a meaningful way, such as saying how many dollars of debt per resident of a country the national deficit represents, that most readers can understand a difficult subject.

If you write about people and always look to see what impact any event or process will have on ordinary readers, you will go far toward simpler and more relevant writing. Journalists, especially those working most of the time with government officials, will be flooded with abstract information, frequently told in complicated ways. Sometimes, economists, educators, doctors and politicians use phrases which they understand but which ordinary people don't. It is your job to interpret this "inside language" so that ordinary people know what it means. You will be surprised when you try to do this, since you may think you know what specific terms like "gross national product" mean. You get a shock when you try to explain in the simplest terms what such a phrase means.

Many powerful people unconsciously or consciously use complex language to help keep them in power. If what they did was really understandable to everyone, then the ordinary citizen would see that what the powerful person does is not so complicated or mysterious. The use of specialized language to protect the "inside," powerful group against understanding by the "outside," ordinary people is very old. In some cultures, for example, the adult men of a tribe even use a special language for subjects of great importance, such as spiritual matters. Women are not supposed to know it or to use it — or in some extreme cases even to listen to it. Obviously, hiding the meaning of what they do gives the "in" group a great deal of power over those left without understanding.

When you as a journalist help everyone understand what is going on, you are helping to spread power in your country. Knowledge is power.

Chapter 6

It is an easy temptation, however, for journalists to get the habit of writing for their sources — often powerful people. The benefits of writing for your sources include keeping them pleased so that they will show you favor and the good feeling you get from being "one of the in-group." Journalists share at least vicariously in power because of their association with important people. This can turn the journalist's head. But if you take your vocation seriously, you know that you have more to do than to write for a small group of important sources in government, business or politics.

Another danger reporters face is writing for the elite group of highly educated citizens in their community or country. If your publication is a magazine which limits its circulation only to college graduates interested in economics, for example, this may be okay. But if you write for a general circulation publication, writing for the educated elite is not fulfilling your duty.

Some reporters believe that simple writing is stupid writing. You will find that to write simply is harder than to write complicated stories. Writing clearly and simply, while at the same time, readably, will try your talents to the utmost.

Of course, you should recognize that there are occasions when you will not be able to write too plainly. This sounds strange, but the reporter sometimes has to observe the fictions of polite society or to go along with not pulling the masks off public officials or others and always exposing their real actions or thoughts. This poses great difficulties for the dedicated journalist. For instance, you may write a story covering a press conference held by a highly placed minister who is announcing a campaign to upgrade the position of women in the nation. But you know that he has helped to keep his own wife subordinate, ill-educated and out of the public view.

If you write a story which exposes the minister for being a hypocrite, it may not be published, or you may be disciplined for writing too plainly, with too much understanding.

Each reporter has to decide how much "truth" his or her readers can take — or more accurately, how much truth is allowable in his or her stories. An injection of too much frankness may bring the reporter's usefulness to an end. This is a dilemma faced by journalists the world over. Of course, if the reporter does choose to write very plainly and truthfully to rip away pretense, he or she must be able to PROVE on solid evidence what is written. It is one thing to say: "The whole community knows this is true, so I can say it without evidence." But it is another — and very dangerous — to write without documentation and necessary evidence.

The way we say things varies somewhat from culture to culture. For instance, some Latin Americans seem to like a bit more ornate language in their news stories. They seem willing to go along with the writer for stylistic reasons. Some Latin American writers feel that to use the same word twice when there is a synonym for it is a crime against style. If they are educated, they feel they should know at least five words for whatever it is they are writing about. But this writer believes such a habit in writing comes from writing for only highly educated classes. Latin Americans who want a mass audience have to write simply. The popularity of tabloid newspapers in Latin America attests to the acceptance of simple writing. The newly educated — or ill-educated — want simple stories with lots of pictures. But the assumption that educated people will always understand or read complex stories is frequently wrong. People often read newspapers to relax. They don't want to have a tough time figuring out what is said, even if they are highly educated.

If you want to be understood, you should first try to find out who reads your publication. You may already have information about this. If it is a general publication, you can obtain information about the overall level of education of your community or nation. If newly literate people are your principal readers, this will make it even more necessary for you to write very simply.

Aids for Writing Simply

The basic journalistic format called the summary news story, which gives the most important information towards the beginning of the story is probably almost universally accepted as the best way to write about something simply. We write

Chapter 6

many stories putting the most important things first because we know that most readers will not read the entire story. If you have something important to say, you don't delay saying it for five minutes.

It has become a journalistic rule for the major portion of stories to be written giving the most important facts first. Some stories may depart from this format, using suspended interest, saving the most interesting thing until last, or they may use a chronological approach. These stories are mainly feature or human interest stories, however.

An aid to saying things clearly is to be sure you know what you want to say before you try to write it. If necessary, do a very short outline, mentally or on paper, before you begin your stories. Every journalist should ask, "What are the most important things about this event or process I am writing about? What is its importance to most of the readers?" Once you have answered this question, you are a long way toward writing simply.

It always helps to use specific examples, anecdotes, direct quotations or personal pronouns and names in your stories. The more personal you can make what you write the more it is likely to be understood.

It should be obvious that if you want to be understood, you will write using words most people know. If you have to use words the general public isn't familiar with, explain these words in the context. If you write in English, you often can say things more simply when you use the Anglo-Saxon root words, rather than the Latin-root words which are more complicated and less understood. This, of course, doesn't necessarily hold true if you write in French, Spanish, or Portuguese where the Latin-root words often are embedded deeply in the language.

If you use short sentences you will be understood better. Scientific studies of English readers have shown that the longer the sentence, the less comprehension there is. It takes more work to make sense out of a long sentence. This writer suspects short sentences are easier to understand in any language.

Writing short sentences doesn't mean that every one you write should read too monotonously. You can vary sentence

71

lengths somewhat and use differing grammatical devices for beginnings. But any time you write a sentence of more than about 25 words you should read it over to see if it is clear. Incidentally, one of the best ways to see if you are writing understandably is to read your own story aloud, or have someone read it aloud to you. If you can't understand it, you'd better make it simpler. Broadcasters have been forced to deal with this reality for a long time. Print journalists can apply the same standards, too.

Some scientists and educators have studied what we call "readability." While much of this research has been done in the writing of English, the main findings probably apply to other languages as well. "Readability" as we use it here means the ease of understanding or comprehension due to the style of writing. It also can be used to describe the interest-level of a story. We are more concerned here with the ease of understanding.

The idea of readability is to try to give the reader written materials which he or she can understand easily. There are tests which have been developed which can show you how difficult your writing is to comprehend. These are mainly U.S. tests, but the general idea will probably hold true. The more complicated your writing, the higher the level of education is required of your reader.

One of the most widely used English readability tests is one developed by Robert Gunning in 1968.[1] It is an easy one to use, and you may want to see how your writing tests.

Gunning calls his test a "Fog Index," meaning that complicated writing is foggy writing. If you are to write simply, you have to clear away the "fog." Here is how to test your writing using the Fog Index:

1. Select several samples of your work. Make each selection 100 words each. Test each sample separately.

2. Find out the average sentence length, dividing the total number of words by the number of sentences.

3. Figure out the percentage of "difficult" words counting the words with three or more syllables (except for proper names, combinations of short, "easy" words, and verb forms which end in -ed or -es).

Chapter 6

4. Get the Fog Index by adding the results of steps 2 and 3 and multiplying the figure you get by .4.

The Fog Index you get gives the "reading level" required for understanding what you have written. This reading level is the level of education required for successful reading of the sample. For instance, if you get a level of "4," that means that anyone with four years of schooling should be able to read the passage. If you get a level of "12," that means 12 years of education would be required. This "education level" score applies to U.S. readers and may not apply directly to your readers. But you can be assured if you get a Fog Index in two digits, you are writing rather difficult-to-understand stories.

There are of course many other things to be considered if readers are to understand us. Some of these are not within the reporter's control but at least should be mentioned. Readers like attractive layouts and pages. They like a variety of graphics, including quality photography, line-drawing illustrations, and the use of color when possible. It is also much easier to read large type. Frequently many newspapers use small body type in order to save paper and space. But your publication may be defeating simplicity and ease in reading if it uses type which is a strain to read. The reporter should at least be careful not to write paragraphs which are so long on the printed page that they discourage the reader.

Almost all reporters have rather large opinions of themselves and the importance of what they write. It is amusing to study a staff of reporters and to see how each of them feels he or she has the most important things to say. We often believe that it is okay for us to write a 3,000-word story when it is necessary for everyone else to be limited to 500 words. The truth is that very few newspaper stories require 3,000 words.

You can say a lot in a few hundred words if you make each word carry its own weight and if you write very carefully. The thing to keep in mind is that very few readers will read more than a few hundred words of your precious prose anyway. Remember the people on the bus or in the waiting room we mentioned early in this chapter: They have many things on their minds and places they want to be. Reading your story is probably not very high on their list of

73

life's important events. Keep yourself conscious of this. Write simply, clearly and readably about subjects in which they have an interest. That's the best you can do, and it is no small accomplishment.

FOOTNOTES

1 From his book *The Technique of Clear Writing* (New York: McGraw Hill, 1968).

Chapter 7
Covering Especially Tough Stories
By Al Hester

The group of convivial reporters, news agency writers and editors sipped on cold drinks, fruit juices or upon good Tunisian wine. The day's official newswriting seminar had been over hours ago. But the group lingered in the hotel room, reluctant to give up the good conversation and comradeship of the day. Outside, a full, silver-bright Tunisian moon came up, and the night breeze rattled in the palm branches. There was a pause in the conversation.

"You know," mused one of the African journalists, "I wish there were some way to do a lot of stories I feel I can't do. You know, the kinds that can upset officials, that really tell people what is going on." Everybody nodded in agreement. Journalists all, whether from the developed world or the developing nations, they were united in trying to figure out ways to cover the "uncoverable."

"Why don't we exchange some ways we cover tough stories?" one asked.

••••••

What follows in this chapter are a few of the suggestions reporters and editors brought up to help others cover major stories of a "sensitive" nature which need to be done. Even where journalists are part-and-parcel of the government press system, they often yearn to be allowed to tell some stories which in one way or another menace highly placed officials, the ruling political party, or other important interests in their country. Frequently such stories don't really undermine a national government or threaten the legitimacy of the party in power.

But it is a fact of life that national leaders, both in developing and developed countries, have contrived to have a near-paranoia that they will be made to look foolish or that the programs they hold dear will be down-graded publicly in the press. Almost every successful journalist, where ever he or she may practice reporting or editing, must develop adroit and tactful ways of getting stories into print about sensitive matters. And it was the consensus of the group of journalists that night in Tunisia at a non-aligned nations news workshop that in almost every country, there are ways to publish stories which at first may seem unprintable.

Of course, in a regime which has absolutely no freedom of expression, the journalist has no latitude in what he or she can write. But most Third World journalists, and even quite a few from the Second, or Socialist, World, say they have had some success in covering the "uncoverable." The readers of this chapter, knowing their own situations, will know whether they may apply some of the methods used. Even if they can't directly use what is suggested, the discussion of how to write about difficult and sensitive subjects may stimulate them to think of new ways to better inform their readers.

The main reason persons in power refuse to let certain stories be done is that they believe such stories menace them in some way. When a reporter or editor believes that a certain story is needful and believes it will be difficult to get in print, he or she needs to ask why it may appear threatening. What is the manacing thing about the story? Few persons like to be attacked with a broadside which questions their authority, intelligence or goodness. Reporters who adopt confrontational tactics and who are plainly hostile are not likely to get very many stories — especially in countries where there are many controls on the press.

News sources and government officials frequently complain that members of the press are mainly in the business of digging up negative, controversial news and have their eyes closed to news at the other end of the scale — news which recounts positive activities and achievements. Journalists frequenly reply that news sources and officials want only self-serving publicity releases which paint them as saints or super-brains. But if we are to consider how to get into print stories about sensitive topics, we must pay attention to the sources of the news and to those who have the power to say "publish it" or "kill it."

Chapter 7

This high importance given to the negative, atypical and aberrational in Western journalism lends some weight to the criticisms by news sources. We will refer to this problem in the chapter on investigative reporting. But we only take time here to point out that many journalists feel they have wasted their time if they have investigated a situation, hoping to find corruption, crime, incompetence or the immoral — and they have instead found honest people doing a good job against heavy odds. This is a strange blindness. It can be highly newsworthy to find upon occasion that government really works, that someone is doing a good job, or that a leader is honest and sincere. Journalists take a cynical view of human nature and reply that the public is only interested in reading who gets caught being a scoundrel, or in finding out that evil rules the day. But positive news can also have readable elements of conflict against adversity of the exceptionally compe-tent or empathetic leaders, or in stories which celebrate the struggle of ordinary people to survive in harsh environments.

Probably the underlying idea of how to cover the "uncoverable" story is to be able to persuade those in power that the stories do not question their legitimacy or the national interest. Getting the sensitive story printed is not easy: you will win some and lose some. But each one printed is a victory.

The reporter must realize that much hostility toward him or her results from the self-righteous attitude of the press which in some countries reserves for itself the self-appointed job of judging who is good and who is bad, and what the best interests of the nation are. The press has the luxurious position of standing back and weighing and measuring performance of government, business, etc., while not dirtying its hands with the hard task of leadership. We can imagine the screams of outrage which would result if the national government, for instance, set up teams of "investigative reporters" to delve into the operations of a major elite newspaper. "By what right do you appoint yourselves judges of how we decide what goes into our paper?" the furious publisher might ask. "Who gave you the moral sanction to sit in judgement of how we serve our readers and advertisers, or how can you tell us what is the common good?"

77

If the reporter or editor can attempt to put himself or herself into the position of persons attempting to run a country, community, business or other organization, this effort will result in more understanding and empathy with these news sources. None of what is said here should mean that journalists should not work hard to do accurate stories about their community and nation. We only say that they must report the scale of human activity, not constantly merely headlining and giving prominence to failures and "bad" news.

The Third World reporter especially needs to approach news-gathering affirmatively with sympathy toward sources, since they are frequently inexperienced in leading and must face many problems more established countries have already dealt with.

The reporter practicing her or his craft must constantly be aware that if sources feel they are being used or manipulated, they are likely to get angry and uncooperative. Each reporter must answer in his or her own conscience about approaches used in covering stories and dealing with sources. Some of the ways mentioned in the rest of this chapter to get sensitive topics into print may border upon manipulation. If the source, or person in power senses the reporter is cold-bloodedly contriving these approaches, everything will be lost. Even in enunciating these methods of dealing with sources there is some danger for abuse. Each reporter must decide which methods are ways to work with sources and those in power.

●●●●●●

Frequently the public official about to deal with a reporter on a story either consciously or unconsciously is asking several questions. When the reporter realizes that these questions lurk in the back of the source's mind, they can be dealt with.

One of the first questions a potential source or government official approving a story must ask is: "Will I lose favor with higher-ups, or will I be demoted, or lose my job?" In some countries, some stories may even result in sources being physically injured or killed. The reporter should always be conscious of such extremely dangerous situations. If the story is that dangerous to the source of information, it may be just as dangerous to the existence of the reporter. There is

Chapter 7

little satisfaction in being a dead hero, even if the story has been told. Hundreds of others will go untold if the reporter doesn't survive to write another day.

When the reporter seeks to do a sensitive story, he or she must be able to come up with answers about why the source should cooperate. Some appeals which can be made include that the story will help explain the work being done by the source or government official. The reporter can also point out, by indirection, that the source's task will be made easier if a thorough story is done about it.

Especially in the Third World, solidly written stories about topics of public interest have educational value. The source may be able to give information through the story that the public badly needs. Many leaders have a strong desire to educate the public about what their program or project is about. The reporter can point out the educational opportunity the story offers.

An approach which is sometimes successful in persuading sources to give information about controversial matters is the assurance by the reporter that his or her story will give the source a chance to have his side of the controversy aired. Politicians especially want to tell their side of the story when the opposition has already had its say.

Some sources or persons in power have a genuine desire to talk about their projects out of altruism. They may truly desire to serve the people well, and a story which accurately reflects their programs or activities will aid their unselfish desire to serve. The reporter or editor is of course a student of human nature. He or she realizes that most persons are a mixture of light and dark qualities, of selfish and unselfish motives. But there is no reason to assume cynically in every case that the source has only selfish motives or is an evil person. After more than 30 years as a reporter, writer and editor, this writer is convinced that virtue exists in about the same proportion among leaders and public officials as it does among private citizens and journalists. No one has a monopoly upon being "good" or being "evil," "smart" or "stupid."

Occasionally the reporter will have to promise the source that his or her identity will not be revealed in a story. If the source believes the reporter can protect what needs to be told without direct attribution, some sensitive information may be forthcoming. But once a reporter or editor promises not to identify a source, that promise must be kept. If it is broken, the source's job or even life may be endangered. The reporter's ability to get further stories from the source whose trust was violated will be nil. Among journalists, reporters or editors who go back on their word to protect sources are considered to be the lowest of creatures. The end does not justify this means.

Third World reporters and editors must be especially careful in promising anonymity to sources about sensitive stories. In the first place, even when such sources are not identified by name, they can frequently be identified because only a few persons may have knowledge of the sensitive matter. Many Third World countries are basically run by only a few hundred persons. It's easy to figure out who "leaked" what sensitive information. In small countries, too, readers (and higher officials) are exceptionally able at figuring out where information may have come from.

The reporter or editor may also keep in mind that he or she may be FORCED to reveal sources of sensitive information. We have seen many instances even in Western countries where reporters have been forced by the courts to reveal their sources or go to prison. There are even more persuasive ways to force reporters to tell where they got information in authoritarian regimes.

Some Third World journalists have had good luck in printing sensitive stories if they emphasize that a situation is a challenge, rather than being a serious problem. The very word "problem" has the connotation of being something negative and threatening to the persons hoping to resolve it. If they are told the reporter wishes to deal with the challenge or opportunity of dealing with a situation, they may be open toward seeing such a story in print. One Third World reporter had very good luck in using this approach to deal with the question of unemployment in his small country. He was able to get government officials to reflect frankly and openly when he posed the question about the challenge of unemployment, rather than about the horrible problem some considered it to

Chapter 7

be. But he was able to convey the needed information in his story.

A rather unusual method used with some success by another Third World reporter is to write graphically about another country's problems. He received permission to do a hard-hitting series about inefficient agricultural production in a neighboring country. His readers were intelligent enough to see that the problems in the neighboring country were almost identical to those in their own nation. The lessons being learned in the neighboring country could be applied in their own nation–without anyone criticizing the Minister of Agriculture.

"Pointing out another country's problems makes you reflect on your own similar problems," the reporter said. "I have also found this method to be about the only acceptable one for writing stories about governmental corruption. It is a no-no to write directly about corruption in my own government. But I am free to bring out the high costs of corruption in bribes and inefficiency — if I use examples which aren't too close to home."

Sometimes it is possible for a reporter or editor to persuade a source or powerful person that doing stories about sensitive subjects is really the source's idea. If the benefits of a reporting project are pointed out to the source or decision-maker, sometimes he or she will go along, even to the point of unconsciously thinking the stories were really his or her own idea. This ploy is probably manipulative. Another more sincere avenue of approach would probably be to see the source and reporter as working as partners to explore a sensitive subject. Reporters and editors need to be able to put aside their own conceits and ego-involvement in order to accomplish this.

Upon occasion, a reporter can disarm hostility in a public official by using what some writers call the Goals-Obstacles-Solutions formula. When interviewing and gathering information, the reporter can first ask the source what his or her goals are. This approach has the advantage of relating more closely with the source. Then, the logical next step is to ask, "If those are your goals, what stands in the way of carrying them out — what are the obstacles?" And finally,

81

many sources will open up when they are asked what solutions might be possible.

Not only does using the goals-obstacles-solution approach help to set sources at ease, it also gives a logical structure to the reports written by the journalist.

This writer has known hundreds of journalists over the years. One common trait many of these have had is that they are somehow mentally conditioned to look for failures of individuals or of the system. To some extent this is healthy, since many public officials and leaders will not call attention to failure. But if the journalist approaches each topic with the assumption that something is wrong, this negative attitude will be reflected in the resulting stories. Quite a few journalists and editors have a "god complex," just as do some leaders. These reporters and editors spout glib, superficial judgements of officials and persons in the news. It is common for us all to project our own shortcomings upon others. The journalist is tempted to do this when working with his or her sources. It is often easier to question the morality of others, rather than to look within our own hearts. It is easier to say what a bunch of incompetents run such-and-such a ministry, when our own newspaper may be botching up things just as much. The mature reporter or editor will recognize these temptations to project our own human weaknesses onto others.

Knowledge of our own shortcomings will help us temper our coverage of the problems of our country or of the lacks in those we deal with. The reporter will hesitate to expect perfection from others when he or she realizes his or her own imperfections.

Journalists have a heavy reponsibility to know themselves. Since their attitudes are often reflected consciously or unconsciously in what they write, they must search themselves for prejudices and biases. They have them, just as do all other persons. Many white U.S. journalists have had to realize they have secretly thought that blacks were dumber, more primitive, less able to advance and to be educated. Journalists frequently grew up immersed in such prejudices. When they began to cover the lives of blacks or problems of racial inequality, they had to become aware that they might have their own burden of prejudice to carry.

Chapter 7

Frequently Western journalists have been liberal politically. It has been difficult for them to set aside their bias to consider conservative politicians. Can the liberal U.S. Democrat put aside bias, writing about the conservative Republican?

In the Third World, can the reporter from the predominant tribe of the country write without bias about members of the minority tribe? Can the black journalist put aside a heritage of wrong-doing at the hands of some white people to see that some white are not evil or exploitive?

As the reporter or editor gains in knowledge of his or her own biases, these can be guarded against in stories. The knowledge that we are fallible, prejudiced beings is soon reflected in our increased understanding and empathy of others facing difficult jobs or situations. Other persons sense intuitively when we ourselves are nonjudgemental or sympathetic in our relations with them. Often the key to doing the controversial or sensitive story is the source's recognition that we will deal charitably with the source's shortcomings or the difficulty in solving a problem.

Some journalists will think that these comments are more appropriate for the psychiatrist's couch or the church service. The psychology of working with sources is given very little attention in the standard reporting texts. These frequently see the reporter-source relationship or the press-government relationship as a black-and-white dynamic. The press is good and all-knowing. The sources, government, private corporation reported upon is the "Bad guy" whose actions must be exposed and condemned. This adversarial relationship is responsible for hostility toward journalists. This writer is constantly amazed that there is even as much goodwill and cooperation shown to journalists. Each reporter working with sources must put aside smugness and self-righteousness that he or she is keeper of the sacred flame of morality and competence.

The reporters who frequently are able to do the sensitive story, or the controversial story, often are the ones who can show understanding and empathy. For every story successfully done by confrontational tactics and hard-nosed journalism, probably ten more are done by non-confrontational efforts and

83

sympathy with the source. This doesn't mean that the adversarial relationship doesn't have its place. The journalist will at times have to get the adrenaline up to do battle. But don't expect to be a winner every time when you irritate or anger those from whom you hope to get stories. More flies are caught with honey than with vinegar.

Chapter 8
Investigative Reporting: Subjects and Methods
By Al Hester

Investigative reporting is a type of journalism which isn't easy to do anywhere. It is even harder to do in many Third World countires, since many of the press systems are an integral part of the national government. Even where the press is separate from the government in the Third World, the idea of actually "investigating" anything meets raised eyebrows.

Part of the skepticism about the ability of journalists to do such reporting, or to be allowed to do it, in the Third World stems from the way we define investigative reporting. Many persons have a picture of the investigative reporter as a combination of crusader, super detective and bloodhound, constantly on the trail of vice, crime, corruption and human frailties.

If we further investigate this stereotype, we find persons think of investigative reporters as hard-bitten, cynical journalists whose main sport in life is "turning over rocks to see what vermin crawl out from under."

All of these stereotypes of investigative reporting have an element of truth in them, but it is unfortunate that the general public and many journalists think of such reporting only in the terms of the exposé always done at the expense of the subjects of the investigation. Investigative reporting can be much broader in scope and can also include interpretative in-depth reporting, in this writer's opinion.

But much of what we call investigative reporting differs in important ways from routine reporting. These differences include:

1. Usually investigative reporting is undertaken with the idea that some action should result, that some change should be made. We will see that sometimes there are exceptions to

this — that sometimes a thorough investigative story might lead to reaffirmation of what is already being done and an appreciation of it by the public.

2. Usually investigative reporting is in a longer format and takes a longer period of time to prepare for, to gather information for stories, and to write.

3. Almost always an investigative reporting effort takes more resources in staff time and in money, since the stories are deemed of more than routine importance.

4. Frequently investigative reporting is undertaken, not just to do a factual report on a subject, but with the idea that change needs to occur, that reforms need to be carried out, or wrongs corrected. Thus, before the project starts, the publication, its management, editors and reporters, all must be in agreement to spend the time and money to do the project.

5. Usually, investigative stories will also involve some special promotion ahead of time to alert readers, some special "packaging" to make the material especially attractive and upon occasion, special distribution of the stories through reprints, special editions or special sections.

6. Usually, more attention is also paid to illustrating the investigative stories with good photographs, drawings, graphs, line-drawings or charts and maps.

7. And usually, the most experienced reporters and editors are usually given the assignment to work with the investigative project, since it is considered one of the most difficult types of journalism to carry out successfully.

8. Almost always, decisions will have to be made by high-level policy-makers at the publication or in a government department to approve an investigative project. This is because the publication in a way assumes a stance either criticizing or approving of the situation being investigated. More is at stake here than routine, non-involved story-writing.

The reporter is frequently expected to come up with ideas for the investigative project. Usually the reporter has a certain "beat" or area for which he or she is responsible for coverage. It is in this specialized area that the reporter will often be asked for ideas for initiative and investigative stories. Sometimes the idea for an investigative story will originate from high-level officials, who will then meet with the reporter and give

Chapter 8

such guidance as is necessary. The reporter is lucky if higher-level officials do not try to second-guess in advance what the outcome of the investigative writing effort will be. Ideally, the reporter, or team of reporters assigned to the project, will be able to plan the project (in conjunction with editors and others) and then gather data upon which to base conclusions.

Reporters must learn quickly that they should not attempt controversial investigations without the sanction of their organization. If they have not received the support of their bosses for the project in advance, pressure may be brought successfully upon their superiors to call off the investigative effort. The reporter who does not have the backing of his or her organization on an investigative project can quickly find the "limb sawed off behind him." Reporters should be warned that if a project backfires, they may find themselves the sacrificial lambs. A high-level official may not be able to take the heat and will say: "Reporter X just got carried away and performed without competence or understanding. We will take disciplinary measures against him. We are so very sorry."

Reporters, too, should be warned that they must proceed cautiously with controversial or sensitive projects. These are the most likely to menace news sources and officials. A good plan is absolutely necessary if time and money is not to be wasted. The reporter, in concert with editors and others, must first of all ask, "What is it that we wish to investigate or find out about?" The next step is to outline as thoroughly as possible questions which will help get answers in the investigation. Next, the reporter must figure out what sources will have the information and whether they will be accessible to the reporter. Interviews, actually observing certain events, doing work for background in libraries or with publications–all of these things may be necessary in order to gain needed information.

The reporter, with editors and others, must also try to estimate whether the investigative task is for only one reporter or for a group of reporters. If more than one reporter is needed, there have to be decisions made concerning who is responsible for what phase of the investigations. It may be that a special editor will also be assigned to supervise the reporters and other editors. If the photographers are to be used, they must be brought in on the planning so they can make suggestions about good pictures. The same is true for artists, cartoonists, or other staff members whose skills will be used.

The reporter, or editor supervising the project, will probably want to draw up a detailed memorandum outlining the theme of the project, the major questions to be asked (as far as can be determined ahead of time), sources to be interviewed, background information to be acquired, and the projected format — for example, a series, a double-page spread, or whatever.

Some estimate of the time and money required must also be made before the project is attempted. Investigative reporting is very thorough reporting and is frequently very expensive. The expense of the project may be too high for the value anticipated. If this is the case, it is better to know beforehand than later in the project.

Goring the Other Fellow's Ox

The following subjects are a mere handful which this writer has heard discussed by Third World journalists as either having been done or needing to be done. Some are more feasible than others.

The first subject might be rather facetiously called "Goring the Other Fellow's Ox." It may be asking too much for the government or a department of the government to investigate itself through its publications. Or it may not be pragmatic for the privately owned paper to investigate certain subjects frankly beyond the pale. This doesn't completely stop investigations, however. There may be areas which are not sacred cows which CAN be investigated. This is not meant to sound completely cynical, but it is a fact of life that some areas will be off-limits, even with the reporter's best effort to show they should be investigated. Why waste time bashing your head against a stone wall? Journalism is truly the art of the possible.

Examples of investigating "the other fellow" include stories about the activities, products or behaviors of foreign organizations. In the Third World, foreign businesses and foreign presences are often looked at with suspicion because of the history of the colonial era. If Western press members feel they must maintain a "watchdog" function to watch for excesses in government power or in big business, the Third World journalist certainly is right to consider investigations of former colonial powers or foreign corporations. Major questions which can be asked might include: Why is the foreign presence in the country? What benefits accrue to the Third World country by the activities of the organization or corporation? Does the foreign presence contribute to employment, to higher standard of living of the Third World country? Are there indications that the foreign activities pose any threats to national sovereignty? Are the major benefits of the foreign presence to itself, or is there equity in the relationship between the outside agency or business and the country in which it operates? What is the pattern of regulation of the foreign interest? Does it operate as a rule unto itself, or is it subject to the laws of the Third World country? Is the management of the agency or enterprise completely in the hands of the foreigners, or does management or control appear to be shared with equity between the Third World country and guest organization? Are there vested interests in the Third World country which profit by the foreign presence at the expense of the majority of the nation's citizens?

Information regarding foreign activities in your country can frequently be obtained from the ministry responsible for regulating the foreign presence. Many countries require detailed information to be filed by trans-national corporations, for example, about profits and losses, taxes paid, employment of national citizens and foreigners, who can buy stock and who has controlling interests in the business. An often-overlooked source for Third World investigative journalists are the documents required of the corporation in its home country or in other countries in which it operates. For example, all major U.S. corporations which sell stock publicly in their operations must file many documents with the U.S. Securities and Exchange Commission in Washington, D.C., which outline quarterly profits and losses, who owns the major portions of stock, recent developments affecting business and earnings of the company, etc. Frequently these are eye-opening to the Third World country in which the transnational corporation is operating.

The above suggestions for investigating foreign presences in a Third World country should not be construed to mean that such outside agencies or companies always operate to the detriment of the developing nation. There may be real contributions made to the economy and quality of life of the developing country. But there also may be abuses and exploitation which come to light.

The operation of foreign charities and religious organizations also may be a legitimate investigative subject. For instance, early in 1985 it was found in the United States that a very large charity organization was not sending much of the money it collected to drouth-stricken African nations. It advertised it was doing a great deal of humanitarian work, but only a dribble of funds and grain reached Africa. African reporters could have worked on this story from their end and called it to the world's attention. As it was, U.S. media became suspicious and even sent reporters to Africa to check on the truthfulness of the charity's claims. African reporters could have been just as active. And they could have enlisted help from their brother and sister reporters in the United States, too. For example, there is a very active and excellent group of reporters and editors called Investigative Reporters and Editors which has its headquarters at the School of Journalism, the University of Missouri, Columbia, Mo., U.S.A. Journalists can join this organization for a reasonable fee and receive publications helpful in reporting and also receive a list of reporters who are interested in investigative work in special areas in which they are expert.

Contamination of the Environment: This is an investigative subject common to many Third World countries. The rapid urban development of capital cities in many countries has seen contamination reach staggering proportions. Sometimes this contamination is the result of hurried and unregulated industrialization. Such industrialization may be by the government itself, by local private enterprise, or by foreign enterprise. It is a sad truth that many

Chapter 8

Third World countries have besmirched their environment because they are in such a hurry to industrialize. They have ignored for many years the heavy price in human suffering and death caused by industrial pollutants and cancer-causing agents. Brazil and Mexico come to mind as countries which have very serious pollution problems occasioned by petrochemical and other industries. It is also true that foreign companies often locate in the Third World to gain the benefits of cheap labor and the lack of environmental protection regulations. Mining enterprises and chemical industries are among the worst offenders.

A related development worthy of hard-hitting investigation is the dumping of dangerous chemical and radioactive wastes in Third World countries. Some poor Third World countries have been tempted to turn themselves into dumping grounds for murderous contamination — contamination coming from wastes shipped in from the developed countries.

The Death of Native Cultures: In some Third World countries, the national government has itself ignored the destruction of minority cultures, offering little encouragement for their preservation. Active discrimination, or passive unconcern, have helped hasten the disappearance of vital cultures. This is also true in some developed nations including the United States, Japan, Australia and South Africa. When these cultures are destroyed, something is lost to the national characrer of the country. The effect of foreign media and foreign business enterprise may also be destructive to indigenous cultures. Military intervention and occupation may also force indigenous cultures to be subservient to foreign interests.

Economic Dependence: This is one of the most pressing problems in the Third World. Although sovereignty has been granted at least in form, a strong dependence upon more powerful nations is still there. What is the nature of this independence? How does the Third World country suffer from it? What may be done to diminish such economic dependence? Who profits by the status quo in the economic arrangement?

91

Handbook for Third World Journalists

The Urbanization of the Third World: This is an overwhelming problem as peasants seek employment in the one or two major cities of the country. What is being done to resolve this problem? What are its consequences? Is there any move to decentralization? What agencies are dealing with it, and how successfully?

Deforestation and Erosion: In many Third World countries, forests are being cut down so fast for cooking fuel that each year the forested regions shrink greatly. The effects of this are devastating — polluted watersheds, erosion, climatic changes, lack of saleable forest products, etc. The turning of wood into charcoal takes gigantic quantities of wood in some countries. Some countries are running out of fuel which poor people can afford.

The Status of Women: In more and more Third World countries women are being accorded higher status and more equal treatment. Often, there is an official policy which states that women should be treated equally. But sometimes officials and private citizens give only token attention to the idea of equal treatment. This is also true of the treatment of minority groups and tribes or classes within the Third World countries. In some Third World countries, the problem of "absent father" must be addressed. Men marry or co-habit with women, siring many children, yet feeling no responsibility for their care. Women are left to support babies without help. This lack of responsibility on the part of men in some Third World countries is very common. The government must attempt to give support to the needy women, or private charities must do so.

Allocation of Funds to the Military: A very ticklish topic for investigation which may be impossible in many counties. But it is true that in many nations, both developed and developing, so-called defense budgets assume staggering proportions while education, health and culture go begging.

You will note that the subjects listed above do not deal with specific events. When we do in-depth or investigative reporting, we often are dealing with PROCESS reporting, rather than EVENT reporting. Much of routine reporting

Chapter 8

deals with recounting specific events. But as we look more thoroughly at society, we begin to deal with processes — ongoing actions, trends, causes and effects. We ask questions such as: What does this whole thing mean? What are its impacts upon society and the individual? What will happen over long periods of time? When we examine the process, rather than isolated events, we can sometimes do more thorough investigation and interpretation. It is not easy work. It is much easier to cover a spot news story or a disaster than to do readable process reporting.

One last suggestion is for the investigative reporter always to keep in mind that he or she must tell the story in human terms. We cannot understand abstractions. We need to visualize people in their daily lives. We need to be able to relate to their very human worries and hopes. Case histories, anecdotes, interviews, oral histories, letting people tell their stories themselves — these are all effective ways of insuring readability and meaning to our stories. Even the most complex stories must be told simply if they are to have impact. Our effort, which is great in investigative stories, is wasted if our ordinary reader cannot understand what it is we are saying.

Qatar News Agency employees discuss operations with U.S. journalism instructor.

Chapter 9
Environmental Reporting
By Mahmoud Abdel Aziz
Reporter, Al Ahram Newspaper
Cairo, Egypt

When Henry Ford succeeded in manufacturing his first automobile, it was a revolution in the means of transportation on the personal and commercial level — an achievement which changed the world. Decades later, scientists have begun to realize that cars also emit harmful gases through their exhaust systems which affect our health and environment.

The issue of protection of the environment becomes a matter of awareness. Most of the projects and problems in the developing countries have their basis in their relationship to the scientific and environmental facts. These facts should be recognized by decision-makers as well as by the public.

The environmental reporter's role is to keep up a continuous effort to inform the public and to make a constant effort to increase this awareness about the environment. The environmental reporter should also have the ability to understand the technical and highly specialized scientific information and to rewrite, or re-edit it in a simple style suitable for the public. This should be done without losing any of the scientific facts. It may be useful and helpful to the environmental reporter to have a scientific background. Photography is another desirable skill for the environmental reporter. Frequently the priority for the assistance of a photojournalist usually goes to covering politics, crime or sports events. Assistance for the environmental reporter comes last. Hence the need for that reporter to take his or her own pictures.

For example, when I covered a story about air pollution at the historical site of the Pyramids and the Sphinx, I had to spend the whole day with the team of researchers of the air pollution laboratory, and I had to climb to the top of the temple near to the Sphinx to get the photographs of the air pollution detectors installed at the level of the Sphinx's shoulder to measure the amount and direction of sand particles blasting at the statue. This would have been a hard situation for the professional photojournalist, who cannot afford the time or the effort, or both.

Among the environmental problems which need special attention in the Third World are the problems of air pollution, especially in the big cities; the manufacture and use of pesticides; and the misuse of agricultural land and forests.

For a long time, competition between economic development and preserving the environment has existed. Everyone seemed in favor of economic development all over the world. In the so-called "Silicon Valley" in California, U.S.A., the first-class, fertile, highly productive agricultural lands were sacrificed to developers to build a base for what was once thought of as the "safe-to-the-environment" electronics industry. But that same industry after a time was proven unsafe, too, and those involved in agricultural food production were forced to move far away to the Central Valley of California where transportation was more of a problem for fertilizers and for getting fresh fruits, vegetables and other products to market. Water was also more of a problem for those who were forced to move.

In India, the Bhopal disaster exposed the problem brought about by some big industrial multinational pesticide companies. They shipped the hazardous and banned pesticides as separate chemical compounds to a developing country, then re-assembled them into a pesticide under another commercial name.

In most of the capitals and large cities of the Third World there is serious air pollution, and this does not get the proper attention or research in an effort to put it under control or at least to lower the level of pollution.

In Egypt, an ancient practice was using mud bricks for building since the time of the Pharoahs. The Nile River annual flood brought a fresh supply of millions of tons of mud and silt, but after the Aswan High Dam construction, mud sediments were deposited in front of the dam, not making their way down the river as previously. Then farmers began

Chapter 9

to sell layers of their topsoil to persons deprived of their usual supply of mud for bricks. This practice led to the loss of fertile top soil in large areas. Others, to solve their housing needs, began to build on agricultural land. But recent laws have banned both practices of building on farm land or excavating topsoil for production of mud bricks. Now there are severe penalties for doing this.

In Colombia, in the vast Amazon forest, illegal coca plantations have had a large-scale development with big profits for laborers and farm owners who produce cocaine in laboratories in the forests. The government has used airplanes and Army troops to fight this practice. But the problem has had a negative effect where there has been damage to the tropical forests, and of course in the exporting of the drug to other countries.

Investigative reporting sometimes could be a suitable way to deal with environmental issues, as when in a report on air pollution in Cairo I had to get the number of cars, trucks and buses running on the streets from the Traffic Department. One can depend on relatives or friends to get information which may not be available through official channels all the time. Then I had to get the chemical analysis of the air quality from the air pollution laboratory at the National Research Center. I also obtained information about the amount of fuel burned in that year from the Department of Petroleum. Then I had to contact the Department of Public and Industrial Health at the School of Medicine of Cairo University to get information about the effect of different components in the gases emitted in the exhaust. These particles included lead, hydrocarbons, etc.

Then I had to go to the Meteorological Department to add to the report weather conditions and how they affect the amount of pollution in Cairo. I also had to obtain photographs and to read about air pollution in science magazines and in reports.

Finally, I had a good report available to me about air pollution problems in Cairo. Other studies which are typical of what a reporter might use for background might include studies about the effect of lead particles on mental processes of workers in printshops using lead and studies about the effect of air pollution on traffic policemen exposed for eight hours daily to air pollution.

In basic environmental reporting, the reporter can get ideas from his or her own interests or personal observations. In 1976, the noise level was very high in Cairo because of traffic jams and the misuse of car horns. This observation which I made was followed by some reading about noise. Also, there was a comparative study available concerning three cities and a remote village in the south of Sudan. In this study the medical team found that noise has had a bad effect on health causing loss of hearing, high blood pressure and tension which can lead to heart disease.

After I had read this information I met with the head of the audio-vocal department at Ain Shames University and took photographs of patients being tested for their degree of hearing loss. After my successful report on noise problems, there was a campaign against noise in Cairo, an indication of the story's impact.

Another field of environmental reporting is that of wildlife protection. Third World countries are the home of many wildlife species which are becoming endangered because of development and expansion of agricultural land uses, taking away their natural habitat. Efforts should be made to preserve the wildlife species and native plants. Mankind should avoid the direct competition with these wildlife species. In addition to the pleasure we receive from watching wildlife creatures, these animals (and plants) are considered to be storehouses of natural genetic materials which could be very useful to the survival of mankind. In Egypt, I wrote several times about the importance of the Ras Mohamed area, the southern triangle of the Sinai Peninsula surrounded by the Gulf of Suez and the Gulf of Aqaba, where the fantastic coralized formations attract divers from all over the world. This area is also the home of the osprey, the fish-catching eagle; and the northern border where mangrove trees growing in the shallow water of the sea have the ability to extract fresh water from the sea water.

Now Ras Mohamed has been declared the first Natural Reserve and National Marine Park in Egypt.

Chapter 9

For environmental reporters, scientific background is an advantage. But an interested reporter can obtain a good knowledge in the field by reading environmental materials published by international organizations, such as the United Nations Environmental Programme. Contact with the U.N. program can put a reporter in touch with the organizations working in the field and with their publications. For example, the international journal for environment and development entitled *Mazingira* is available.

The environment is a multi-disciplinary subject, which includes science, medicine, public health, meteorology, engineering, city planning, economics, and many more facets of man's life. So a stream of continuous awareness is needed until we reach the point of the optimum development of our resources with a minimum disturbance to the environment. Having that awareness is the job of the environmental reporter.

Handbook for Third World Journalists

Chapter 10
Coverage of the Role of Women in the Third World
By
Edith Nkwazema, News Agency of Nigeria, and "Fatima" (Anonymous) of Algeria

(EDITOR'S NOTE: This chapter is the work of two women journalists in the Third World. One prefers to remain anonymous, but she is an experienced journalist, as is Edith Nkwazema. They were invited to give their views of the situation of women in the Third World and how journalists may explore this important question.)

Press Coverage of Women's Role in the Third World, with Special Reference to Nigeria
By Edith Nkwazema

Records of women's active participation in political, economic and social development of Nigeria date to as far back as the pre-colonial days.

History records the activities of Queen Amina of Zaria who fought battles and subdued difficult men in the northern part of the country. Also Mrs. Fumilayo Ransome-Kuti, mother of Nigeria's Minister of Health, Prof. Olukoye Ransome-Kuti, used her state base to organize women into pressure groups that campaigned against oppressive colonial rules and later against the Alake of Abeokuta in Oyo State who had to abdicate his throne due to pressure mounted against his rule by Mrs. Kuti and her group.

Mrs. Kuti never compromised her quest for fairness to women and humanity.

Also by 1929 Aba women in the old eastern Nigeria organised a riot against the colonial administration for urging women to pay tax. Other women in the east joined.

At Opobo, women also took to the street to support the tax protest and 50 of them were shot dead, many wounded. The shooting order was given by the colonial masters when the women refused to call off their protest march.

My grandmother was arrested and imprisoned during the riot, she said.

To the average Nigerian woman, the need for recording of events of history and more importantly reporting on daily bases, woman's activities in all spheres of their lives cannot be over-emphasized, for if the brief historical background of women's activities given above had not been recorded, I wonder how those activities would have been passed on authentically from generation to generation.

So there is dire need for recording on daily basis the activities in Nigeria, Africa and indeed in the Third World today.

Problems include lack of commitment and sustained interest both on the part of women and the press.

Women's waning interest is apparently due to lack of properly defined roles. Many have still not realised that their roles of traditional wives, mothers and home keepers have been expanded into bread winning in addition to the original role.

Many are still hiding under the canopy of their husbands, not wanting their economic roles to be overtly acknowledged in order not to upset the status quo, that is by admittng publicly that the women are complementing their husband's economic role in the family.

But sometimes when the women do realize that they have added more to their traditional reponsibility, they hardly find time to come together to discuss how best to meet the challenges of their added responsibility. Heavy household chores and at times lack of funds to back up their demands militate against group interaction among women to discuss and proffer solution to their problems.

Again the women are divided among themselves — literate versus the uneducated. Under such a situation, presentation of a common front is difficult. The educated ones find it almost impossible to descend from their ivory towers to offer hands of fellowship to their illiterate sisters.

Chapter 10

The illiterates dismisses the "acadas" as wayward, overbearing "tarmagants."

Where such a dichotomy exists, there's no common meeting grounds that would positively draw press attention.

How about the press? Are they any better? Certainly not, in some cases.

Many male journalists still dismiss women's activities with a wave of hand — regarding them as another forum where women gather to discuss people, latest fashion and both imaginable and unimaginable trivialities instead of discussing issues and ideas as men would do. But whether men discuss more important issues at gatherings is subject to debate. Personally, I sometimes find coverage of women's activities boring because they are sometimes not properly organised and could be rowdy irrespective of their education and high positions. But this does not mean that I do not respect fellow women. I very highly do. What happens, I guess, may be that women even prefer me to cover their activities. Still, many women of substance feel very confident when I cover their activities.

Also, sometimes coverage of women's activities face the problem which arises from the reporter's inability to pay his way to the rural areas where the majority of our women dwell.

However, investigations have revealed areas where women want more publicity. They include health, entertainment, shopping guide, drama and fashion.

Theresa Oguibe, woman editor, *Nigerian Statesman*, says, "Newspaper managers don't encourage heavy stuff for woman's pages in the Third World but also in the First and Second Worlds."

She adds that this accounts for many women's magazines in America and Western Europe.

But she points out that she has been lucky that in all her career as a woman editor even for big national papers like the *Daily Times*. She says she has had a free hand to a large extent in choosing topics for her page and she has discussed women's problems, politically, economically, socially and otherwise. When the need arises, she says her managers have also drawn her attention to some other areas that would be of interest to women.

Unaku Ekwegbalu, woman Editor, *Daily Star*, adds, "your colleagues and employers cannot push you around when they realize that you know your job."

She also expressed satisfaction with the amount of freedom she has in running her page.

She points out that she commissions, accepts and publishes articles of interest to women while the editor picks out news items for the paper.

The two women editors agree that women want to read, watch and listen to stories and articles on health because the family revolves around the women who would want to be armed with all facilities that would enable their families as well as how to cure them when they are ill.

But do female journalists have any set in the profession? In the history of the media in Nigeria, there were no women in the profession.

But thank God that today conscious efforts are being made to cater for women affairs. The radio, TV and newspapers now have departments aimed at focussing on women's problems and proffering suggestions. Unaku Ekwegbalu says again, "This has been yielding fruits. Also our universities are turning out more and more female mass communication graduates to handle these programs."

In fact, she stresses that there is great need for these departments to discuss the role of women because until an understanding is arrived at, many women will find it difficult to bring out their best.

Traditionally in the Third World, women are supposed to be seen, not heard; but now the Third World woman has added to her original role to be a bread winner. She is no longer what is termed in Igbo parlance "Oriaku," that is "she who has come to enjoy wealth," but "Okpataku", that is she who has come to join hands in the struggle to create wealth. And women should see themselves as such and their husbands should recognize their effort to contribute to the total well-being of the family.

In the race to define this role the educated ones should descend from their ivory towers to accept their uneducated or half-educated sisters. They should both work hard and ask questions to know more about what is going on around them

Chapter 10

and also make their own contributions.

It is unfortunate that social problems that wind around tradition and religions exist, for example when a man wants to be selfish he starts quoting what the African culture says about marriage and goes ahead to acquire about 20 or 30 wives depending on the weight of his pocket. But we must take solace in the fact that many educated men don't believe in displaying their wealth by the beavy of women they have around them with uncountable number of children. They know that they owe humanity more than that and should strive to live up to that expectation.

Among Moslems, religion poses a serious threat and Theresa suggests that female Moslems should interpret the Koran instead of leaving it to males who would always weave in elements that would take the women away from the scene to their own (women) detriment.

The interpretation of the Koran has always put Moslem women away from the public glare into the purdah. Although Latin American women are hard-working, poverty drags them down. There's low literacy rate among Asian women — all these need to be highlighted by the press and solutions put out.

There's a need for permanent employment for married women, for a fight for women to get maternity leave with pay to uplift womanhood. In Nigeria, anyway, married women are permanently employed.

It will be recalled here that during the last republic, one of the Governors in Nigeria — Chief Michael Ajasin of Ondo State restored full leave allowance to women in his state.

Also in Nigeria the fight for equal working opportunity is yielding fruits and within the academic community in Nigeria women are being recognized although the number is so insignificant compared to males.

The first women vice chancellor was appointed last year (1985) for the University of Benin State. She is Prof. (Mrs.) Grace Alele-Williams.

But the National Council of Women's Society (NCWS) under the leadership of Hilda Adeferasin says that this is not enough and that many more women should be appointed to policy-making positions.

To the Third World female journalist who has a vital role to play in developmental journalism, her philosophy should for ever be, to fulfill the ideals of journalism that is, to educate, entertain and objectively collect and disseminate news. She should also mobilize women for execution of government policies on rural development for the improvement of the majority of the people of these countries who live in villages and hamlets without roads, light, water and more painfully, without food.

I hope that the stigma of waywardness and insubordination many a time labelled on the female journalist should be dropped as she cannot help smiling sometimes against her will, and also cannot help being inquisitive, courageous, bold and sometimes stubborn to make sure that she puts out news or feature packages that would meet the needs of the masses.

••••••

Women in the Algerian Society
By "Fatima"

There is hardly any coverage of the role of women in our society. After independence, the Algerian Revolution set the stage for a "new start" for the women's movement in connection with the big political projects announced (communal reform, agrarian reform, etc.).

Women have played an important part in the national liberation struggle. As early as 1966 the General Union of the Algerian Women (UNFA) evolved a document in which it insisted on the need for involvement of women in the political life of the country, including their involvement in decision-making. However, a change in leadership of the organization resulted in a shift in the treatment of women, focusing from that time onward on "the social problems" as linked to "the problem of women." From that time, the organization's thrust has been toward the participation of women in the achievement of the socio-economic projects and political mobilization.

Chapter 10

Between 1975 and 1978, major projects were launched. Two main areas were highlighted: the need for institutional reforms to meet "the new requirements" and the working out of a new ideological doctrine.

On the doctrinal level, and on the occasion of the debate of May, 1976, on the draft bill of the National Charter, a particular effort was made for the formulation of the "problem of women." In its contribution, the women's organization developed the theme of emancipation through participation in the building of the nation. When the People's National Assembly was set up, the principle of equality between men and women was consecrated in it.

Yet the contradiction between the official text and reality is perceptible. The political speech on women as reflected by the media seems to have as a primary concern to show the conformity of the political ideology with the ambient ideology of the soicety. There is a refusal to break with certain values and concepts. Certain stereotypes are even picked up by the press, particularly the idea that woman is primarily a source of danger for the society, a force capable of upsetting the social order if not guided and in the absence of defensive values.

Women have achieved some progress on the path of emancipation since independence, thanks to free education and access to employment; but they are still confronted, from an ideological point of view, with the cultural images developed about them. Women are suspected of not taking into account the national realities and of being under the sway of foreign cultural influences whenever they demand parity of status with men at all social levels. The weight of tradition in our country is heavily against women. Even the so-called respect for women is respect for their capacity to suffer and bear the burden of humiliation and insult.

In our male-dominated institutions, even when women break the barriers and go up the ladder, they are still not accepted as equals of their male counterparts merely because some narrow-minded persons are desperately trying to perpetuate an order that has been banished by the revolution. Moreover, women's work whether it is manual, artistic or intellectual is always ranked less significant compared to their domestic role.

The fact that working women are overburdened with their double-load of responsibilities, at home and at work, is considered as something natural, an additional sacrifice, a sort of price women have to pay because they are willing to reconcile between the fundamental role assigned to them: that of housewives and mothers, and their role as workers. If it is a necessity, women's work is neither linked to an idea of autonomy of women vis-a-vis the group nor to individual freedom.

The working women are compelled to abide by the norms and stick to the socio-cultural values of the group and the national community. Women here are constantly grappling with backwardness. It is not easy to get rid of the secular weight of taboos and preconceived ideas. Besides, the deficiency in the educational, cultural and health institutions and the problem of transport are making it increasingly difficult for women to conciliate between their professional work and their work at home. Instead of pin-pointing these problems, the media increase the working women's difficulties by permanently culpabilizing them by singling out and exalting their role as mothers and housewives. Presently, our women are so exhausted and disillusioned that they have lost interest in work and life in general.

One of the problems that need to be brought to light by the media is inequality between men and women in facts. Though the fundamental texts [for the National Charter] state that men and women are equals, it is not so in facts. How can women enjoy their rights as citizens when they live under tutelage at home? Women are considered as minors all their life. They are not considered at all as individuals. If women procreate so much in our country and in the Third World, it is because prehaps procreation is the only role that is being acknowledged. This is why speaking about family planning is definitely speaking about the status of women. The demographic policies followed by the country have started questioning the role of women as mothers but only from an economic point of view. The subordinant status of women is almost universal. All societies are male-dominated. There is no society in the world where the two sexes are involved in all sectors, political and professional, and participate with the

Chapter 10

same weight in decision-making. The problem has a causal link with historical, religious, social and economic factors.

The number of women working in the media has increased over the past few years. There are not many women editors but there is a large number of women reporters who are doing very well especially because they are young and more pugnacious than their elders.

Efforts are being made to improve the situation of women, notably by women. Roundtables have been held for some time to discuss the the role of women. These roundtables are organized by university teachers, journalists and cadres (women). This group of women also publishes a magazine entitled *Presence Femme*, created to enable women to express their views. The first roundtable held recently had "women and employment" as a theme. The debate which took place was both interesting and enriching. Extremely important points discussed include: the prospects of women's employment in future in the aftermath of the economic crisis, the necessity of vigilance for the safeguard of the gains wrestled by women, etc.

A new women's magazine entitled *Djamila* will be published soon. Named after three heroines of the national liberation war, *Djamila* is a socio-cultural magazine created to fill a cultural emptiness. Many interviews have been conducted with women to find out how they want their magazine to be, what they expect from it, and the questions they want it to tackle, etc. Our women have hitherto read French magazines that are not conceived for them. *Djamila* tries to live up to the expectation of women and deal with issues that are a matter of concern for them. It will be a forum for discussion.

Women who choose a career working in the media confront many difficulties. A woman reporter is first viewed as a woman, and like in other sectors of activity, she is segregated and restricted. It is very difficult for a woman to distinguish herself in an area thought to be reserved for men. Women are sent abroad very rarely, if at all, for the coverage of international events. Women reporters are not promoted as quickly as male reporters even when they are competent. Besides this, they are restricted by their husbands who are not very helpful or understanding. Husbands often object to their wives working at night or going on assignment inside or outside the country and this acts as a brake upon their career. Women reporters should be persistent in their fight for the equality for women. They should never give in. They have to conquer all the hurdles standing in the way of their emancipation. A change in the subordinant status of women will come from women. Besides, sweeping economic and social changes must be brought about in Third World Societies. The uplifting of women is contingent upon how far women are prepared to go to wrestle for their rights. In our Third World societies engaging in an unremitting struggle against under-development, it is imperative that women realize their full potential and share in the burden and ecstasy of building their countries, not as subordinates, but as equals of their male counterparts.

Chapter 11
Beyond Reporting
By Wai Lan J. To

The role and career of the Third World journalist has many facets. With limited human resources and economic necessity, having more than one job, and media cross-overs are facts of life. A young person might aspire to be a journalist, or a writer, and start as a reporter for a newspaper, or for a radio station. Soon the reporter might also work parttime for a magazine, or a researcher or scriptwriter for a television station. Maybe the very same reporter would be promoted to the post of editor, or become an information officer, or even go into politics. The dedicated journalist/writer often realizes that he or she has to be flexible and adaptable in her or his creative pursuits, as well as in serving the community; and reporting is only one of the many ways towards the goal of national and economic development. This chapter offers a few examples and observations on the alternatives beyond reporting.

Literary Journalism

As press systems in the First World tend to move more and more towards investigative and interpretative reporting, some journalists feel that the scope and craft of journalists should also be expanded. "Literary journalism" is a result of their efforts.

The term " literary journalism", in the West (in this case, mainly in the United States) can be traced back to the 1930s. In 1937, Edwin H. Ford compiled a bibliography of literary journalism.[1] In the foreword, Ford wrote that the term "Literary Journalism," conceived for the purpose of the bibliography, might be defined as writing which falls within the twilight zone that devides literature from journalism. The literary journalist is the link between newspaper and literature:

111

The reporter gathers news which indicates political and social trends. The editorial writer comments upon such news, but within restricted compass. And, when these political and social trends or situations have sufficiently permeated the thoughts and feelings of people generally, they provide the materials from which the mind of the artist creates literature. Through the medium of sketch or essay, of the literary or humorous column, of verse or of critical comment, the literary journalist refashions and evaluates the world about him. The literary journalist is the writer who is sufficiently journalistic to sense the swiftly changing aspects of the dynamic era of our times, and sufficiently literary to gather and shape his material with the eye and hand of the artist.

Today, "literary journalism" refers to a journalistic style, a non-fiction literary genre, which combines the skills of interpretative reporting with the technique of fiction writing. Literary journalism may be in the form of newspaper feature, magazine article and book; and its principal functions are still to inform, to entertain and to educate. However, the writer has more freedom in style and in the presentation of his materials, and as a result, it makes the writing more enjoyable and reading more interesting.

"Literary Journalism" is also another term, a more appropriate term, for the controversial "New Journalism"[2] of the 1960's. No matter what it is called, fundamentally, the literary journalist is still the artist who puts events and phenomena into perspective, and interprets and evaluates the world around him. As Norman Sims in the anthology, *The Literary Journalists*, points out, literary journalism was not defined by critics. The writers themselves have recognized that their craft requires immersion, structure, voice and accuracy. And along with these terms "a sense of responsibility to their subjects and a search for the underlying meaning in the act of writing characterized contemporary Literary Journalism."[3]

Ford's early concept on literary journalism seems to apply to a lot of the prevailing journalistic practice in Third World nations.[4] For example, there is a similar genre called "journalistic literature" (*Bao Gao Wen Xue*) in China. The Chinese genre of literary journalism would also include stories

Chapter 11

based on facts and personal accounts of historical events [5] and exemplary works of revolutionary journalism [6]. However, the concepts, and techniques of Western literary journalists may provide reminders or new directions for the Third World journalist trying to find a more creative and expressive platform for his or her ideas.

The literary journalists's "craft," as Norman Sims said, requires immersion, structure, voice and accuracy.

Immersion. In researching the story, in order to put everything in the proper perspective and be as accurate as possible, the literary journalist would gradually become immersed into whatever he is working on. To do so he or she has to spend weeks, months and even years in research, depending on whether the writer is preparing an article or a book. For example, John Mills spent five months walking a dangerous beat in New York with a detective to write about his life, in "The Detective;" Truman Capote spent five years researching a murder case in Kansas to recreate the events prior to and after the crime, in *In Cold Blood*; Tom Wolfe spent seven years interviewing and corresponding with pilots, astronauts, and their wives and relatives besides delving into the archives of NASA to write about the courage of test pilots and astronauts in *The Right Stuff*. Some even get more personally involved and become participants in the event. George Plimpton joined the Detroit Lions football team to write about the experience of a pro football player (*Paper Lion*); Hunter S. Thompson rode with the Hell's Angels motorcycle gang and nearly got killed in the effort (*Hell's Angels, a Strange and Terrible Saga*); and Norman Mailer was a participant in the Pentagon March, a demonstration in Washington, D.C., in 1967, (*The Armies of the Night*).[7]

In this case, time is a main constraint for Third World journalists. Third World journalists may not be able to spend as much time on a single story or topic as their counterparts in the West; however, the enthusiasm and sheer dedication of literary journalists would serve as a reminder of their own quest, and provide inspirations for story ideas, and possible angles or treatment.

113

Structure. While the structure of journalism is usually chronological, literary journalism usually takes a more complicated form which is closer to a short story or fiction novel. Literary journalism, as Tom Wolfe summarized, (or "the New Journalism" in Wolfe's terminology) employs the technique of the fiction: scene by scene construction; dialogue; point of view — sometimes through interior monologues of characters; and status of life descriptions — such as clothing and mannerisms of characters, details of objects in the environment. In this case, the journalist's eye for detail, keen sense of observation, interview techniques, and language skills would be the prerequisites.

To Wolfe, these are the very devices that give the realistic novel its unique power. Since most of the 20th Century novelists (in the West) have abandoned their "calling" as "chronicler of history" and devoted their efforts to myths, fables and forms, the writers of New Journalism has taken their role to become "secretaries of society." [8] Wolfe's own work and others' collected in the anthology, *The New Journalism*, serve to illustrate the variety of techniques and the wide range of subjects of the genre, as well as the changes in styles of living in the United States in the '60s.[9]

The writing styles and some of the techniques advocated by "the new journalists" which seemed innovative at the time have since become standard features of magazine writing. For example: the anecdotal opening, is one of the many devices to capture the interest of the reader by, essentially, telling a story; capturing the personality of the interviewee by describing his mannerisms; and in character writing, by imitating the style and manner of speech or writing of the subject character in the story.[10]

The architecture of a story of the literary journalism genre would be thematic, or in the form of flashbacks, story-telling, or even the flow of stream-of-consciousness (as in most of Hunter S. Thompson's works[11]). Also, by using narrative devices such as association, juxtaposition, and parallel narration, the writer can provide a social and even historical interpretation to ideas and events.

The journalist in developing nations is in effect a "chronicler of history." With the progress of development, or

Chapter 11

sometimes the inconsistency of govenment policies, or even the instability of political systems, issues may disappear and problems become more complex. The writings of the journalists soon become records of the changing times before any history book can be written.

Voice. The most controversial aspect in literary journalism would be "voice," as most of the works in the genre are subjective and interpretative by nature. Since conventional journalism in the First World espouses "objectivity," literary journalism lends itself for criticism.

In the Second and Third Worlds, the voice of the journalist or narrator is the most important aspect of mass communication. As most media are either state-owned, party-affiliated or geared toward national and economic development, subjectivity often is a fact of life and not an issue for debate. Standards for fairness and balance in the treatment of subject matters would also vary from country to country. Yet, in the Third World, the voice of the journalist is vital: the voice of the journalist (and/or the media), in the form of analytical and interpretative information as well as informed opinions would be invaluable to a public confronting the currents of modernization and upheavals of development. This information and opinion would help the people to make sense of their complicated and everchanging environment.

Accuracy. The main difference between literary journalism and fiction is that literary journalism is presenting FACT using the writing techniques of fiction . That does not mean that the facts are fabricated. The criterion is accuracy. The journalist can be imaginative in the way he or she may present and interpret the facts. That does not apply to inventing facts or taking literary license by twisting the facts to suit the journalist's purpose. In this respect, the note book, or the tape recorder, would be vital to the journalist. In reconstructing the scenes of events or dialogues of characters, the literary journalist would have to be very careful and double check his notes and tapes.

As John Hersey, who had years of experience working with *Time* magazine, wrote that there is no such thing as objective reportage: "Human life is far too trembling-swift to be reported in whole. The moment the recorder chooses nine facts out of ten, he colors the information with his views."[11] What the literary journalist is trying to be is to acknowledge this fact, and be subjective in trying to make sense out of this complicated world. Instead of just reporting the facts, he tries to analyze what is going on, to interpret what it means and get at a larger "reality."

Journalism and Fiction

When the journalist witnesses some great events or makes some observations that cannot be fully expressed in a newspaper or magazine feature, writing a book — non-fiction or fiction — may be an answer.

When novelist Truman Capote first published *In Cold Blood*, he insisted that it was not journalism but a new literary genre he had invented — "the non-fiction novel."[12] No matter what it is called, the work structures like a novel, reads like a realistic novel, but the events in the story actually happened. It is the writer's reconstruction of something that happened, and his re-creation of incidents before and after the event. In Capote's case, it evolved around a murder and its victims and suspects. A book of this nature, in efffect, is a case study, and a vehicle for social comments.

Hunter S. Thompson took the idea even further. Thompson fused facts and fantasies and created "Gonzo Journalism," a highly interpretative and personally involved style of writing in the New Journalism stream. His parodies on the 1972 U.S. Presidential campaigns are witty and entertaining, but damaging for the political candidates when they appeared in *Rolling Stone* at the time.[13]

Some writers in the Third World could only envy the luxury of such freedom of expression enjoyed by their First World colleagues. Sometimes when the social and political climate of a country is such that the reporter runs the risk even in straight reporting — merely relating the facts and quoting the exact words of officials — let alone interpretative reporting. To fuse facts and fantasies like Thompson would be highly dangerous for the writer.

Chapter 11

However, journalists and other media workers in such adversities are usually very resourceful. They know how to circumvent the scrutiny of censors and work around the constraints. They write fiction, stories in the form of fantasies, fairy tales and fables. They use cartoons, popular songs, chants and verses, and wall posters. The puppet theatre becomes the stage of the voice of the repressed, and street drama, the vehicle for social and political criticism.

And then, there is nothing wrong with wanting to write a novel or produce a play to express some personal observation of life in general, or even just to suit the creative fancy of the author (provided that the author is an ethical and socially responsible person).

In any case, journalism is not necessarily "more true" than fiction.[14] It may be, as Hunter Thompson in his more serious moments wrote, that both "journalism" and "fiction" are artificial categories, and that both forms, at their best, are only two different means to the same end.[15]

Humor

As media workers, we often remind ourselves that we have this serious responsibility of informing and educating the public we serve; and we tend to forget that, at times, something in the comic mode might be more effective in getting the message across.

Humor is more than a literary or narrative device for the creative person operating in a repressive environment: It is the pretext and platform of expression, and the weapon of the oppressed. For those who have lived under colonial rule or experienced oppression, reading between the lines and sensing the meanings of parodies and allegories is a means of survival.

As Emir Rodríguez Monegal said, "... laughter is the weapon of the oppressed used to parody and destroy the solemnity of their oppressor."[16] He points out that the tradition of laughter has a long history in Latin American literature, whether be it Peruvian, Brazilian, Argentinian or Mexican.

117

"Satire in colonial literature," wrote Monegal, "is both a literary technique and way of preserving personal integrity."[17] To him, the greatest Latin American writer of the 20th Century is Jorges Luis Borges, "the parodist, deconstructionist, reducer of philosophy to science fiction and metaphysics to fantastic literature." And among those writing in the Latin American tradition of laughter include Nobel Prize winner, Brazilian, García Márquez (*One Hundred Years of Solitude*), and the Cuban author, Guillermo Cabrera Infante (*Three Trapped Tigers*).

Latin American literature is only an example of the functions of humor. The form or medium of expression may vary from culture to culture, yet laughter is an essential part of our lives. At times, humor — in the form of irony, satire or parody — maybe "the smiler with the knife under his cloak,"[18] for the underdog and repressed. It can also reduce tension and provide relief for the man or woman after a day's hard work in the fields, at home, at the factory or office; or the catalyst of self-reflection for a society enjoying economic and political stability.

Telenovelas

As laughter can be a useful tool, entertainment can be the vehicle for important messages. That does not mean to negate the functions of news stories, or radio and television newscasts and documentaries. The traditional categories of media entertainment, such as humor columns, cartoons, as well as radio and television dramas can complement development programs, such as government health programs, or bringing about tribal understanding or religious tolerance among the people.

Latin American countries, especially Mexico, are quite successful in developing the potentials of television entertainment, through *telenovelas*, in connection with national development. The *telenovela*, a type of soap opera developed during the 1950s and '60s, is the dominant genre in Latin America.[19] In a study on the success of *telenovelas*, Rogers and Antola pointed out that: themes emphazising upward social mobility, and educational and other goals in addition to entertainment are among the characteristics of *Telenovelas* compared to their U.S. equivalents. And, these series capture the mass audience, unlike soap operas in the U.S. where viewership is predominantly female and mostly for day-time viewing.[20]

In the 1970s, in Mexico, Televisa produced several popular *telenovelas* with themes toward social improvements in line with government projects and campaigns. They include: *Come with Me* (*Ven Conmigo*), fostering adult literacy training; *Accompany Me* (*Accompáñame*), promoting family planning; and *Let's Go Together* (*Vamos Juntos*), combating child abuse. According to the production company's research, during the year in which *Accompany Me* was broadcast (1977), the number of family planning adopters in the country increased by about 560,000; and the research also suggested that the one-year broadcast of *Come with Me* helped to bring about an increase of enrollment of about 1,000,000 in adult literacy training classes.[21]

These Mexican educational soap operas were inspired by the success of an extremely popular Peruvian *Telenovela* of the 1960s, *Simple Maria* (*Simplemente María*).[22] A modern Latin American version of Cinderella, *Simple Maria*, is about a girl from the slums who started as a maid of a rich family, and eventually becomes a fashion designer due to hard work and her ability as a seamstress. The show made profits for the production company, and enhanced the sale of sewing machines in Latin America; and it also presented an educational theme that contributed to national development.[23]

The results of the Mexican programs, in turn, have inspired other Third World countries to produce educational soap operas. India, for example, has produced a series, *The People* (*Hum Log*), on family planning. It was broadcast on prime time in mid-1984 and enjoyed a rating of 90, which sparked other production of soap operas. Other Third World countries are also planning to use this form of entertainment to promote national development goals such as family planning and the equality of women.[24]

What attracted the audience to these educational soap operas, according to Rogers and Antola, is their fast-moving and emotionally charged stories: "the audience see them

119

primarily as entertainment."[25] These programs do not try to "teach" family planning or literacy. They are subtle and indirect in their approach. For example, in *Accompany Me*, the characterization of positive and negative role models was based on family planning behaviors promoted by the Mexican Government; and *Come with Me* tried to show low-income individuals participating in adult literacy classes.[26]

From the Mexican experience, we can learn that something educational does not necessarily have to be solemn and dead serious. As William C. Miller advises aspiring script writers: an issue is often a challenging starting point for a script; however, the writer should moderate his zeal and avoid being too obvious or preachy.[27] Subtlety is the key. In producing educational radio or television dramas, the message has to be natural to the context. Also, any transformation or conversion of the characters — for example, when the reluctant traditional farmer finally decided to participate in a farming program advocated by the government, or the mother forgiving the daughter for marrying someone from a different social class — should be developed with a plausible story-line and in line with the personality of the character(s).

Narrative Structure

Men have been telling stories since prehistoric times. The tribesman tells of the boy who walked bravely into the jungle, ready for his first hunt... The old man under the banyan tree speaks of the young man who journeyed to a distant mountain to seek training from a legendary master swordsman. The *Wayang*[28] master enacts the tales of the *Ramayana* in which the hero with the help from the gods defeats the evil forces of the demons.... No matter in what form or medium, past and present, there is always a purpose, a message somewhere. Myth, legends, folktales, fairy tales, fables and parable, whatever the term or category it may be, they are subtle carriers of moral codes, values and models of conduct of the culture.

In many ways, as journalists, writers, or writers/producers of radio and television programs, we are essentially "story-tellers." First, our editors, publishers, producers, or

Chapter 11

production managers, have to "buy" our story. Then we have to attract and retain the attention of our audience. Otherwise, whatever jewels of wisdom we have would be lost. As communicators working in a developing nation or newly independent country, we are constantly working to establish a solid cultural identity in our work to counter the possible "cultural invasion" of the developed countries. Maybe one of the solutions would be to get the inspiration and foundation from the different narrative and poetic forms of the our indigenous culture. We need to know our audience, as well as what is the best way to reach them, and how to get our messages across. It is important to examine the prevailing social climate in order to understand the mindset of the people. However, it is also important to be retrospective and to learn from history and traditions. Proverb and parables are useful tools for putting certain ideas into the perspectives to which the audience can relate. In the realm of beliefs and moral values often the answers are embedded in myths, legends, folklore and popular stories at the time. They can provide ideas for the theme and contents of stories, or used as analogies to news events or description of news makers. At the same time, they are valuable sources of ideas for presentation and form.

Child development and cognitive psychologists in the West have found that children gradually develop the sense of the plot of the story during grade school (primary school according to some school systems). They expect a certain sequence from the story they heard. They would tend to understand and recall a story better if the stories are told in the "ideal order."[29] Maybe structural and content studies of the stories in folklores, myths, popular arts, and/or other narrative forms would be an appropriate topic for communication researchers in Third World countries. For example, Dan Ben-Amos, in a comprehensive study of African folklores, defines the functions of different forms of African tales as well as proverbs and riddles, and discusses studies of other researchers concerning the structure of African narrative forms.[30] Perhaps different "ideal forms" can be developed to suit the audience of different cultures.

121

Ethics

There is no entertainment per se. There is always a purpose behind the story-telling. It depends on whether the story is used for a good cause or for selfish reasons. It is understandable that in a community where illiteracy prevails, the word becomes more sacred; and in a nation which worships technology, voices from the radio or images on television would be expected to embody the truth. A journalist or media person should caution against being wrapped up in the myth of his or her own power. Ethics is personal and cultural. There is no fixed standard as there is no definite way to present a message. To have an open mind and continue to be receptive to the needs of the community and ideas for solution; to serve humanity and maintain personal integrity are some of the appropriate guidelines. Just remember that in a world of flux and instability, people tend to look to the media for information, guidance, inspiration and moral support. Words of encouragement, and stories that spreads the ideas of tolerance, understanding, love and peace, and generate hope, are some of the motifs.

FOOTNOTES

1 Edwin H. Ford, *A Bibliography of Literary Journalism*, (Minneapolis, Minn.: Burgess Publishing Company, 1937).

2 When the térm "the New Journalism" caught on in the mid-1960s, it referred to writings by magazine journalists such as Jimmy Breslin, Gay Talese, Terry Southern, Tom Wolfe, Joan Didion, Gail Sheehy and Tom Gallagher, among others; and novelists such as Norman Mailer, James Baldwin and Truman Capote. Because of its subjective style, and some of the writers' unconventional usage of the English language and punctuations, "the New Journalism" is also called "personal journalism," or " parajournalism" by its critics.

3 Norman Sims, *The Literary Journalists* (New York: Ballentine Books, 1984), pp. 3-25.

4 See Chapter 3 of this *Handbook* for a survey and comparison of the press systems and news concepts of the First, Second, and Third Worlds.

Chapter 11

5   Sometimes fictitious names of people and geographical locations are employed to protect the anonymity of the people involved.

6   See Chapter 5 of this *Handbook* for a definition of Revolutionary Journalism.

7   Features and excerpts can be found in Tom Wolfe, & E.W. Johnson, Eds. *The New Journalism* (New York: Harper & Row, 1973).

8   Tom Wolfe, "Part One: The New Journalism," in Tom Wolfe, & E.W. Johnson, Eds., *The New Journalism*, pp. 3-37.

9   Wolfe, & Johnson, *The New Journalism*. Features and excerpts contained in the anthology are some of the finest examples of the New Journalism and literary journalism. Subjects covered range from the lifestyle of film stars and celebrities, to life of servicemen in Vietnam; from sports to politics; and from high society to racial conflicts.

10   Roy Paul Nelson, *Articles and Features* (Boston, Mass.: Houghton Mifflin Company, 1978).

11   In James E. Murphy, *The New Journalism: A Critical Perspective*, *Journalism Monographs*, vol. 34 (Lexington, Ky.: The Association for Education in Journalism, 1974), p. 23. Murphy's work contains a comprehensive history and analysis of the style and criticism of New Journalism.

12   Wolfe, p. 37.

13   The series of articles was later published as *Fear and Loathing: On The Campaign Trail '72* (New York: Fawcett Popular Library, 1973).

14   John Hellmann, *Fable of Facts: The New Journalism as New Fiction* (Urbana, Ill.: University of Illinois Press, 1981), provides an analysis of the different perspectives on journalism and fiction.

15   Hunter S. Thompson, *The Great Shark Hunt* (New York: Summit Books, 1979), p. 106. Some of Thompson's examplary works are published in the collection, apart from the ones contained in Wolfe & Johnson's anthology.

16   Emir Rodriguiz Montegal, "Tradition of Laughter," *Review: Latin American Literature and Arts*, vol. 35, July-December, 1985, p. 3-6.

17   Ibid.

18   Ibid., Monegal quoted one of Borges' favorite passages found in Chaucer.

19 Everett M. Rogers & Livia Antola, "*Telenovelas*: A Latin American Success Story," *Journal of Communication*, vol. 35:4, Autumn, 1985, pp. 24-35.
20 Ibid., p. 30.
21 Ibid., pp. 31-32.
22 Ibid.
23 Ibid., pp. 33-34.
24 Ibid.
25 William C. Miller, *Screenwriting: for Narrative Film and Television*, (New York: Hastings House, 1980), p.146.
26 Rogers & Antola, p. 30.
27 Miller, p. 146.
28 The *Wayang Kulit*, the shadow play, is a popular art form in Malaysia and Indonesia. Sacred tales from the Hindu epic, the *Ramayana*, are transmitted through the *Wayang* masters (called *Tok Dalang*) who hold high esteem among the people.
29 Aimée Dorr, "When I Was A Child I Thought As A Child," in S.W. Withey & R.P. Abeles, Eds., *Television and Social Behavior: Beyond Violence and Children*, (Hillsdale, N.J.: Lawrence Erlbaum Associates, 1980), pp. 191-230.
30 Dan Ben-Amos, "Introduction: Folklore in African Society," in Bernth Linfors, Ed., *Forms of Folklore in Africa: Narrative, Poetic, Gnomic, Dramatic* (Austin,Tex.: University of Texas Press, 1977), pp. 1-34.

Chapter 12
An Overview of Editing
By Warren K. Agee

Editing is a responsibility shared by many people on a newspaper. It begins when a reporter polishes a story before turning it in. It ends when final errors are corrected just before the edition goes to press — even afterward if deadlines permit. Between these events subeditors practice their art. How well they perform determines the difference between a highly readable, perhaps exciting, issue and a mediocre one.

On newspapers everywhere an editor-in-chief sets policy and supervises the entire operation. Depending upon the size of the newspaper, one or more subeditors — the managing editor, city editor, wire editor, news editor — decide what will and will not go into the publication. It is the copy editor, however, who makes the final checks for quality and accuracy, and it is upon his or her work that this chapter is focused.

Duties of the Copy Editor

Basically, the copy editor performs the following functions:

- Searches for factual errors and corrects them.
- Guards against contradictions and edits the story to correct them.
- Corrects errors in punctuation, grammar, spelling, figures, names and addresses.
- Makes the copy conform to the newspaper's style.
- Condenses the story, making one word do the work of three or four, making one sentence express the facts contained in a paragraph. Trim the story to the space ordered.
- Guards against libel, double meaning and bad taste.
- Dresses (decorates) the story with typographical devices, such as subheads, as may be indicated.

•Writes the headline for the story.
•On some newspapers writes captions for photographs and other art work related to the edited stories.
•After the edition has gone to press, examines the paper closely as a furtther protection against error and makes corrections if deadlines permit.

Obligations of the Copy Editor

The copy editor owes primary obligations to the reader, the newspaper and the author of the story that is edited.

The reader: The copy editor should be aware of the common characteristics of age, educational level, standard of living and life styles of the newspaper's principal readers, and edit stories accordingly. In many Third World countries a newspaper's readers are urban, educated and middle- to upper-class citizens; they can grapple readily with reasonably complex stories. Even so, the best newspaper writing is simple and direct, and the copy editor should labor to make it so. The application of modern journalism's dictum, "Make it clear, and make it interesting," will serve not only the better-educated readers but also will help expand readership to those who have shunned newspapers because they cannot read well and understand the stories they contain.

Equally important is the copy editor's obligation to the reader to improve a poorly written story or one that does not immediately draw the reader into it. A common failing is a story with a traditional, matter-of-fact lead (intro) that could be replaced with a narrative or anecdotal account containing a strong human interest element (impact, conflict, oddity, for example). Often such elements are "buried" in the story. It should be the operating premise of every newsroom that editors do more than correct grammar and write headlines, that their main function is to improve stories.[1] The reader will be the beneficiary of such a practice.

Coping with life conditions is a universal human problem. The copy editor should be alert to shape as many stories as possible so as to emphasize ways in which readers may benefit by reading them, other than for news or entertainment. How may I reduce taxes? How may I protect my family against disease? The copy editor often may reorganize a story to stress information that induces higher readership and helps people cope with such problems. The effort to help readers identify with the news is the first principle of good editing.[2]

Many copy editors have discovered that they do their finest work when they keep ONE reader in mind rather than edit for a large, anonymous audience.

The newspaper: The copy editor has been aptly described as the conscience of the newspaper. He or she stands in the doorway between the reporter and the reader of the story as the final arbiter of style, taste and quality. Upon such standards rests, in large part, the credibility of the newspaper. Consistency is the goal in such matters as capitalization and abbreviation; the use of titles, punctuation, spelling and grammar; the selection of type faces for headlines, and the like. Readers lose confidence in a newspaper that lacks high standards and consistency in such matters.

The author of the story: The obligation that the copy editor owes to the author of a story is to improve it in every possible way without damanging the writer's individual manner of expression. The newspaper is the product of many people and one of its chief attractions is the variety of its context. The copyeditor must resist creative urges of his or her own and alter stories only when abolutely necessary. The rush of handling numerous stories and writing headlines normally negates against reworking.

The Qualities of an Editor

Whether in a developing or developed country, the qualities that should characterize an editor remain the same. Harold Evans, former editor of the *Times* of London, discusses these qualities in his book, *Newsman's English.* As adapted for a seminar for journalism educators, they are as follows:

•human interest qualities of sympathy, insight, breadth of view, imagination, sense of humor.

- An orderly and well-balanced mind, which implies judgement, sense of perspective and proportion.
- A cool head, ability to work in an atmosphere of hurry and excitement without becoming flustered or incapable of accurate work.
- Quickness of thought, coupled with accuracy.
- Conscientiousness, keenness and ruthlessness, rightly directed.
- Judgement, based on well-informed common sense.
- A capacity for absorbing fact — and fancy — and expressing them in an acceptable manner.
- Adaptability — the power (whatever your feelings) of seeing things from the reader's point of view.
- Knowledge of the main principles of the law of libel, contempt and copyright.
- Physical fitness for a trying, sedentary life that takes its toll of nerves, sight and digestion.
- Team spirit — a newspaper is one of the more striking products of cooperative enterprise and effort.[3]

The Tools of Copy Editing

The tools necessary for copyediting are universal. They include a dictionary, stylebook, thesaurus, encyclopedia, grammar handbook, atlas, book of familiar quotations, telephone directory and city directory. Most should be within easy reach of the copydesk; others may be in the newspaper's library.

All these tools are necessary because the copy editor must check the factual content of stories; memory cannot be trusted. Frequently, they may be used to embellish a story.

In the numerous developing countries where newspapers are produced by the traditional "hot lead" method, the copy editor requires other tools as well: a heavy-lead pencil, eraser, scissors, paste pot to use if portions of copy are pasted together, and perhaps a typewriter. Copy is edited by hand and the headlines are written either on separate sheets of paper or at the top of the stories. The stories and headlines are set into type and proofread. The type then is placed into forms for stereotyping or direct printing on presses. In many countries, offset printing, based on lithography, is replacing this process.

The use of video display terminals (VDTs) is spreading around much of the world. On newspapers with such equipment, a story is written on a VDT and transmitted to appropriate editors and hence to the copydesk. There the copy editor calls up the story, edits it, writes a headline and indicates the type size and column width of text and headlines by striking the proper symbol keys. Finally, the copy editor touches a key and dispatches the story to the phototypesetting machine.

Newspaper publishers in some countries, finding video display terminals too expensive, have purchased electric ribbon typewriters for their newsrooms. Using white bond paper and carbon-film ribbons, reporters write their stories on these typewriters. The stories then are scanned by an optical character reader (OCR), also known as a scanner, and converted into computer language to drive a phototypesetter. Because corrections must be neatly typed between typewritten lines, a time-consuming process, reporters and editors have found that the introduction of OCR technology discourages editing.

Editing the Story

A copy editor should first read the entire story to gain a full understanding of what the writer is trying to say. Then, much like the sculptor with a chisel, the editor begins to chip away clutter and redundancies. Other writing faults also are corrected as the story is gradually shaped into sharply delineated form.

Clutter: It is rare that a story cannot be simplified. With a keen eye, the editor deletes extraneous words and phrases, constantly asking : "Are these words necessary? Can the story be told as well, or better, without them?"

The straight declarative sentence — first the subject, then the verb — serves comprehension well. Unnecessary phrases, clauses, adjectives and adverbs reduce understanding.

Most sentences should be short — like this. For variety and rhythm, and perhaps necessity, however, adjoining sentences may be longer and more complex — like this. Many editors follow the guideline of ONE IDEA TO A SENTENCE. Care must be taken, however, to avoid choppiness and changing the meaning of what the writer wanted to say.

Superfluous attribution is another example of clutter. Statements, of course, must be properly attributed to the source, but some writers insert a constant "he said" element that can be eliminated.

Redundancy: Just as in a conversation, many writers say almost the same thing twice, or more, to make sure the point is not lost, but more likely because of deadline pressure or sheer carelessness. The alert copy editor notes repetitions and deletes them.

More commonly, redundancies take the form of one or several unnecessary words. Examples: "little baby," "young boy," "future plans," "completely destroyed."

Clutter and redundancy are only two examples of the many writing faults for which the copy editor also is responsible if they are not corrected. Every country has its idioms, slang terms, cliches, bureaucratic jargon and the like that infest otherwise readable stories. The principles of proper writing, however, are universal. An American dictionary once erroneously defined "journalistic writing" as "hasty writing." Even stories that are composed in a hurry can be grammatically and structurally sound; if not, good editing will make them so.

Creating the Headline

After checking copy for accuracy, clarity, conciseness, unanswered questions, consistency of style and tone, the copy editor's next task is writing a headline.

Functions of the headline: A good headline:
- Attracts the reader's attention.
- Summarizes the story.
- Helps the reader index the contents of the page.
- Depicts the mood of the story.
- Helps set the tone of the newspaper.
- Provides adequate typographic relief.

Chapter 12

Headlines have been called the display windows of the newspaper. But they are more than that. They also are a major source of information. Few people have the time or desire to read everything in the newspaper. By perusing the headlines, they quickly learn "the top of the news" and can decide which stories, including features, merit further attention.

Varying headline sizes and styles and the placement of stories, whether on the first page or elsewhere, serve an indexing function — they convey to readers the relative significance of the news. Gothic headlines generally indicate serious stories; the use of italics and typographical devices such as boxes generally indicates that the story is printed primarily for its entertainment value rather than its significance.

Headlines also:

•Compete with each other in enticing readers to their stories. A good story may be largely overlooked if its headline fails to attract the reader.

•Provide the ingredients of an attractive display package. The headline in all its various forms is essential to assembling pages that are eye-catching, balanced and attractive.

•Lend character and stability to the newspaper. The consistent use of familiar headline families and styles gives the newspaper a relatively familiar and welcome personality.

•Sell newspapers, especially those editions that are purchased mainly at newsstands or in sidewalk boxes.

Writing the headline: The skills necessary for successful headline writing include: 1) accurate perception of the story; 2) a vocabulary that is both broad and deep; 3) a sharp sense of sentence structure; and 4) a keen eye for ambiguity.

The headline must be drawn from information near the top of the story and key words selected that will fit the allotted space. Normally, a noun is followed by a verb and both are placed in the top line if at all possible. Label (non-verb) headlines may set the appropriate tone for some stories, usually features. Except in feature headlines, articles and most adjectives and adverbs are eliminated.

131

The copy editor should try to capture the flavor of the story. Short, simple words are preferred. Overworked headline words, known as HEADLINESE, should be avoided. Abbreviations generally should not be used. Phrasing the headline in the present tense is almost always essential. A person's name should be used only if he or she is prominent. Verbal phrases and nouns and their modifiers, as well as infinitives and prepositional phrases should not be split from line to line. Only single quotation marks should be used. The headline should be specific, not vague. Most important, it must FIT, its length neither too long nor too short for the allotted space.

Editing Wire Copy

The clatter of press association teleprinters, delivering stories hour after hour with almost relentless precision, stirs a sense of subdued excitement in newsrooms throughout the world. The dispatches typed out by the automatic keys of these machines on continuous rolls of paper represent the world of action, under datelines of Beirut, London, Lima, Moscow, and a thousand other cities.

Gradually, however, these teletypes are being replaced by computers and VDTs, just as the teleprinters replaced the Morse dot-and-dash circuits. In the most technologically advanced newsrooms, dispatches are fed directly from a news service computer into the newspaper's computer, for editing on a VDT, at a much faster tempo than previously. High-speed printers are available for backup in case the newspaper computer fails.

Largely because of poor revenues and labor union resistance, as is true, for example, with most daily newspapers in Portugal,[4] hundreds of dailies have not yet been converted to the new technology. They still receive dispatches via radio or landline teletype circuits at approximately 66 words per minute. In some offices the dispatches are accompanied by perforated teletypesetter tapes. These tapes are used to drive a linecaster or phototypesetter, thus eliminating the need for redundant keyboarding of wire service copy. This chapter section focuses on the handling of traditional teletype dispatches.

Chapter 12

Each press association usually divides its flow of news into P.M. and A.M. reports, or cycles, the former for afternoon newpapers and the latter for morning papers. These reports always begin with a "budget," or checklist, of the most important stories that are to be transmitted. The budget represents a summary of the basic stories then available or known to be forthcoming during the next few hours. Usually it contains 10 or 12 items. The news editor is thus able to plan the paper's makeup and to save space for stories most likely to be run.

Major stories that break after the budget has been delivered are designated FLASH, BULLETIN MATTER and URGENT. Such designations, which differ in terminology in various parts of the world, alert the news editor to important, newly developing stories.

News editors receiving the dispatches of more than one press association select the stories that they like, check facts in one story against another, or combine the best elements of each. In the latter case, the credit line is removed and replaced with an overline such as "From Wire Services."

As the dispatches arrive, either in their entirety or in "takes" of successive parts, including new leads, inserts and corrections, the editor places them in stacks or in folders according to their anticipated use or location in the paper. Copy for inside pages is handled first with the principal news items held for possible later developments. Each story carries notations showing its priority, number, slug (one or more words denoting its content), dateline, lead, and ending matter indicating, among other things, the source and time the dispatch was sent.

The copy editor handling a certain story is given all the dispatches that pertain to it in order to mould the copy into finished form. If the copy is printed in all capital letters, the copy editor marks each capital and small (upper- and lower-case) letters, and then it is edited the same as local copy. The copy editor, if required, trims the story to fit the allotted space, then deletes errors and polishes the copy, and writes the headline. In some countries, such as India, this process is known as "subbing" (sub-editing) and "copy tasting."[5]

133

Editing perforated teletypesetter tape is difficult and time-consuming, so generally the full story is set and any superfluous copy discarded. Otherwise, changes must be made manually with the use of editing or proof symbols. Newspapers using this system surrender much of the flexibility in editing that they have with other forms of copy.

One important task of the wire editor is to check incoming copy for news elements that may be localized.

In computer-to-computer news delivery systems, the wire editor may first receive an abstract of the cycle's complete offering, transmitted to the newspaper's computer at speeds of 1200 words per minute. Through computer commands, complete stories may then be called to the editor's VDT screen. The editing is much simpler than with teletype copy: Rather than inserting new leads and corrections, the editor receives updated stories in their entirety. Split computer screens make it possible for editors to combine portions of stories from different news agencies.

FOOTNOTES

1 From remarks by K. Finkel of the *Dallas* (Texas) *Times Herald* at Journalism Educators Seminar sponsored by the American Press Institute, Reston, Virginia, U.S.A., October 7-12, 1984.

2 Floyd K. Baskette, Jack Z. Sissors and Brian S. Brooks, 3rd edition, *The Art of Editing* (New York: Macmillan Publishing Company, 1982), p. 14.

3 Adaptation distributed at Journalism Educators Seminar sponsored by the American Press Institute, Reston, Virginia, U.S.A., October 7-12, 1984.

4 Warren K. Agee and Nelson Traquina, "A Frustrated Fourth Estate: Portugal's Post-Revolutionary Mass Media," *Journalism Monographs*, February, 1984, p. 19.

5 Indian Institute of Mass Communication, *A manual for New Agency Reporters* (New Delhi: Allied Publishers Private Limited, 1980), p. 84.

Chapter 13
Broadcast News Writing
by Vernon A. Stone

(EDITOR'S NOTE: Although both Chapters 13 and 14 use many U.S. examples and illustrations, there is much solid information for those preparing broadcast news throughout the world, and for that reason, at the request of Third World broadcasters, we have included Dr. Stone's excellent material. Chapters are used by permission of Dr. Stone.)

Who Cares?

There seems to be an inverse relationship between need for improvement and efforts toward improvement in broadcast news writing.

Good writers of the U.S. networks like John Chancellor of NBC, Walter Cronkite of CBS, and Harry Reasoner of ABC seek always to polish their news copy. Edwin Newman of NBC has been described as a "superconscientious stylist" who pores over old scripts "searching out cliches and useless words to further hone an uncluttered style."

Bad writers, on the other hand, often think they're pretty good and may argue that matters of style are unimportant. In conducting clinics for television news practitioners often badly in need of help, I have found them eager for tips on shooting better newsfilm, doing smoother interviews, and dressing up production. But they tend to show little interest in improving the basic techniques in which they are most deficient — writing.

Even the news writing on the networks is sloppy at times. But at the local level it is often terrible. Drive through any part of the United States listening to local radio and watching local TV news, and you may wonder what ever happened to literacy. Is clear, precise, listenable writing obsolete?

The guidelines that follow were written on the assumption that a few men and women working in broadcast journalism or aspiring to do so still are not content to be mediocre.

135

Rather, they strive for excellence and, like Edwin Newman, are willing to exert the effort necessary to achieve it.

Self-criticism may not be enough. The guidance of a capable and critical editor or teacher is important for most beginners. They tend to be impressionable, and shoddy practices observed in an old pro (often a half-competent hack) easily rub off. Colleagues at other universities have observed that their weaker broadcast journalism students often include some who have picked up bad habits by working at a radio or TV station with low standards. It may be difficult for them to unlearn what the late Allan Jackson of CBS called "atrocious ideas and styles for writing and news programming."

William Small, vice-president and news director of CBS News, has said that "good writing, rare as it is, will always be the heart of what television tries to do." Small and others in leading radio and television news operations are always looking for news men and women who can write well. They won't go long without jobs.

Effective broadcast news writing has its rewards, not the least of which is the self-satisfaction from communicating clearly.

Writing for the Ear

You may find radio and television news writing a refreshing change from newspaper style. Broadcast copy not only permits but requires the form of expression which is probably most natural for you — namely that of speech. We learn to speak before we learn to write, and we talk a lot more than we write in everyday communication. The naturalness of the spoken word is too often lost when the writer thinks in terms of narrow columns of type and rules of journalese left over from another era. As a broadcast writer, think instead of how words and their combinations sound. Talk the news as you write it.

We don't go around talking in awkward newspaperisms like the dangling attribution. In telling someone about a speech, it's doubtful that you would say:

> Out-of-state students are vital to the University of Wisconsin, Gov. Patrick J. Lucey said today.

Chapter 13

You might say:

    Governor Lucey said today that out-of-state students are vital to the University of Wisconsin.

or:

    Governor Lucey says out-of-state students are vital to the University of Wisconsin.

Read the three versions to someone and you'll see the difference. The last two — in broadcast news style — read easier for you and come across better for the listener. Those are the objectives toward which most guidelines for broadcast news writing are directed. The copy should be (1) easy for the newscaster to read and (2) easy for the listener to understand.

Since newspaper copy is often difficult when read aloud, should you do as one manual suggests and "forget everything you have learned about newspaper writing"? Certainly not. Most of the fundamentals of effective news writing apply across the media. For example, the story must be accurate and clear. The words used should be precise, the grammar correct, the sentence construction easy to follow, and the story organization logical. The lead should draw attention to the main element of the news story. Thought units placed together should indeed fit together. Modifiers should be close to what they modify. Long phrases or clauses should not separate the subject and the verb. And a clear writer must be a clear thinker. Such elements underlie all effective verbal communciation and are basic to good writing in all media.

Any sloppiness in thinking or writing which makes a newspaper story hard to follow is even worse in broadcast news. Readers may be able to go back and re-read until they figure a newpaper story out. But listeners normally cannot call back the newscaster to run through it a second time. In broadcast news, a story must be perfectly clear and easy to understand the first — and only — time it's heard.

It may also help to remember that the person on the other end may be only half listening. His or her attention may be

137

divided between the news program and rush-hour traffic, homework, the morning paper, conversation, or a combination of such distractions. Much as newspaper readers scan headlines to decide which stories they want to read, listeners may be catching only key words which alert them to those stories they care to pay attention to. This means that if the lead does not clearly cue listeners as to the nature of the story, they may not start paying attention until most of it has been missed.

With these general considerations in mind, let's go to some specific guidelines to make the news easier to read aloud and easier to listen to.

Focusing the Story

The shotgun approach of reporting every fact in sight won't work for broadcast news. There's not time for it. For example, when commercial time has been deducted from a 5-minute newscast, seldom is time left for more than 50 lines of copy. (The average newscaster reads 15-16 lines a minute.) And you may want to get 8-10 stories into those 50 lines. This means that you must exercise news judgement and report only the most important element of those stories.

More than your newspaper colleagues, you must be selective. You must focus clearly on the most important part of a story and not bog down in secondary details. Listeners can effectively take in only a limited number of different bits of information in a given period of time. So don't try to cram too many facts into a story. It's better to do justice to one or two main points than to try to communicate a telescoped digest of six or eight points which overload the listener and may actually communicate nothing.

At the same time, avoid the kind of headline treatment that leaves listeners wondering what a story was all about. Some backgrounding or elaboration is often needed, even if it crowds out some new information. Again, you serve listeners better with one report that says something than with two reports which are so sketchy that neither makes much sense.

Chapter 13

Writing from Wire Copy and Newspapers

Never parrot a story from a news wire or a newspaper. Get into it with your own approach and tell it in your own words, using the source copy only as raw material. Too many so-called rewrites are in fact little more than re-typed excerpts. Although such is discouraged by the wire service, their broadcast stories often consist of the first two or three paragraphs of a newspaper wire story with a word or two changed here and there. Many of them read well enough and may be appropriate for the wire service, but this is not broadcast news writing.

Especially if the original reads well, as it often does, you may find it hard to break away from its wording. The trick here for most people is to lay the source copy aside and write from memory, referring to the wire or newspaper story only for exact quotes, names, and such. This forces you to put the news into your own words.

Learn to scan the source copy, looking over it quickly and dwelling only on the highlights. If you read all of it carefully, you may find no time is left for writing newscasts. To be a competent news writer or editor, you must come to work well backgrounded on the news. You won't have time to get that backgrounding from the present day's file, and it's not available on the radio wire anyway.

So prepare yourself by reading newspapers, magazines and other materials to keep you up to date on everything of importance in the world about you. Journalists who know only what they read on the radio wire (a service that prints out headlines and little nutshells all day long) are only superficially informed and not really up to writing or editing a newscast.

If you don't understand a story, there's a good chance that many listeners may share your bewilderment. The lazy writer will copy an explanatory clause or phrase from the wire without knowing what it means. The good writer will figure it out and express it in a way that's perfectly clear.

What of writing from a newspaper without permission? It's done in hundreds of broadcast newsrooms every day. It need not constitute a copyright violation, though it often

139

does, and many stations get by with it. News — information about events — is not copyrightable, but authorship — the wording of the original — is. When the broadcast writer uses the newspaper story only as a source of information and then turns away and writes a story in his or her own words, that's all right in most cases. But when the wording is the same, or even substantially the same, as that of the newspaper, the station is guilty of copyright violation or a similar transgression. And now and then, it's pleasing to note, one of them gets caught.

A word of caution. If you broadcast a libelous story you've picked up from a newspaper, your station will be just as subject to legal action as the newspaper. When you trust a secondary source, you're on your own.

Telling It Clearly

There's no substitute for the direct style of sentence and story construction. When you have the story in mind, tell it in a straightforward way. Avoid putting participial phrases or dependent clauses at the beginning of sentences. If the main element is qualified by some "ifs" or "buts," present the main element first and then get into the qualifications.

The lead should call attention to the main element of the story and should not be crowded with too many facts. Don't try to cram all five Ws and the H (Who, What, Where, When, Why and How) into the lead. You'll lose the listener through overload.

The first words of the story should clearly cue the listener to what it's all about. A fragmentary sentance may make a good scene setter. For example:

> Labor trouble in New York tonight. The city's transit workers voted to strike unless...etc.

But use this approach sparingly. It can get montonous and also consumes time unnecessarily. A sentence is the best lead for most stories. Example:

> Transit workers in New York City voted tonight to strike unless...etc.

Chapter 13

Avoid leading with direct quotes or questions. A direct quote may make the listener wonder for a moment or two whether the words are those of the newscaster or someone else. The question lead sounds too much like a soap commercial or game show.

Make your points one at a time. Wrap up one aspect of a story before going to the next. For example, tell what the President said about Vietnam, then what he said about taxes, then his comments on politics in California, etc. Don't jump back and forth from one to another. This forces too many reorientations on the listener.

The general usually requires fewer words and is easier to grasp than the specific. So when specific identifications, figures, and such are not essential to the story, skip them. In the New York labor story, we could give the exact name of the union local, but most listeners couldn't care less. "Transit workers" conveys the meaningful information.

The indicative tense, when appropriate, usually carries more impact than the subjunctive.

Heard on a radio station:

> The Board of Regents decided that course-credit would be withheld for any student who refused to be photographed for an I-D card.

Better:

> The Board of Regents decided that course-credit will be withheld for any student who refuses to be ... etc.

Avoid long, involved sentences. Flesch says they should average about 17 words. Actually, sentence length per se is less important than a logical sequence of thought units that flow easily from start to finish of the story. But unless you're a real master with words, chances are that your copy will start bogging down when the sentences start getting long.

A troublesome sentence can often be improved by breaking it into two or more thoughts, or sentences.

Bad:
> Senator Gaylord Nelson, speaking before a meeting of University of Wisconsin Young Democrats in Madison yesterday, said the United States should stop the bombing of North Vietnam.

Better:
> Senator Nelson says the United States should stop the bombing of North Vietnam. Nelson spoke at a meeting of Young Democrats from the University of Wisconsin in Madison yesterday.

Because small mouthfuls are usually easier to handle, a prepositional phrase after a word often comes across better as a modifier than an adjective preceding it. "Members of the United Nations" reads better than "United Nations members."

Clauses tend to be more forceful than verb-form phrases.

Awkward: *Weekend* reports of China's Mao Tse-Tung having suffered a stroke...

Better: *Weekend* reports that China's Mao Tse-Tung had suffered a stroke...

As limited as we are for time in radio and TV, a certain amount of repetition or redundancy can help the listener. Repeating a key name or other important element in a later sentence is a service to the listener who starts paying attention late. It can also make the story clearer, even for the attentive ones. Be sure the antecedent or a pronoun is clear, and if in doubt, repeat the name. Never use "the latter" or "the former" — the listener cannot look back to see which came first and which last. As for "respectively," forget there's such a word.

The "ing" verb forms are overused by some broadcast writers. Direct verb forms often do the job better.

Heard (re plane crash):

> ...landing 20 feet off the runway and settling in the mud.

Chapter 13

Nothing wrong with that, but more direct is:
> It landed 20 feet off the runway and settled in the mud.

For some on-the-air reporters, the "ed" sound comes across easier, stronger, and more effectively than "ing."

Names and Identifications

Don't lead with unfamiliar names. They're too easy to miss. Set the listener up for them by leading with identifying information about the person.

Examples:
> A Gainesville attorney — William Hardin — announced today...
>
> A University of Georgia student — Diana Jones of Atlanta — has been named to...
>
> Senator Olson has appointed an administrative assistant. He is William Finnegan, a...

It's all right to lead with a familiar name like President Carter, Senator Proxmire, or Governor Lucey. For that matter, such public officials usually carry a title before the name, so it's still a matter of going from identification to name.

Middle initials of most newsmakers are omitted for broadcast. Indeed, if a person is very well known — like Carter, Proxmire, and Lucey (in Wisconsin) — the first name is usually skipped. If you're sure most members of the audience know the first name, omit it. Otherwise, include it. The middle initial should be included if it appears needed for exact identification, as with an accident victim or a suspect in a crime.

The newspaper form for ages — John Jones, 30 — should usually be avoided. The standard broadcast approach for years has been 30-year-old John Jones. If in doubt, use this style. But now and then it's good to hear someone break

143

the monotony of the standard treatment of ages. For example, with a separate sentence — Jones is 30. Or, in a series, the newspaper form may be the most practical: He has three children — John, 6... Edward, 4... and Susan, 2. When is one form more appropriate than another? When that's how you would say it in talking with someone.

Attribution and Quotes

Attribution should be made clear and should be placed before what the person said. This is part of direct oral expression: who - said - what. As noted at the start, the dangling attributions so common in newspaper stories make for unnatural speech patterns. Do not use them.

Use quotes sparingly. The paraphrase or indirect quotes is usually preferable. You can often say it more concisely than the news source, and the exact words are seldom so important that you gain by presenting them as such. If a dairy spokesman tells you that "the price of milk is going up" and those are the words you use in the story, the fact that they happen to be exactly the ones the spokesman used is too trivial to justify making them stand out as a direct quote. Such quotes only clutter you copy.

Direct quotes are usually taken from a larger context and may not be as clear as a paraphrase.

Bad:

>Democratic Chairman Lawrence O'Brien said in Washington today, "A year and a half of attention directed to the Southern Strategy has not worked for this administration."

Clearer:

>Democratic Chairman Lawrence O'Brien said in Washington today that the Nixon administration has directed a year and a-half of attention to the Southern strategy... and it hasn't worked.

Chapter 13

If the exact words are so colorful, meaningful, or controversial that you feel you should make them stand out as a direct quote — do just that. Remember that the listener cannot see the quotation marks on the copy. If the newscaster is proficient in oral interpretation, the handling of direct quotes is not much of a problem. But for safety, in case he or she is just reading words, make the quote stand out as such by the way you write the copy.

The method used in the early days of radio — "quote... unquote" — has fallen out of favor in most newsrooms, probably because few people talk that way. Some acceptable methods now in use include:

...what the senator called "gross deception..."

The senator put it this way: "A nation divided..."

The President said — and these are his words — "That's the ugliest thing I ever saw."

Said the governor: "We'll win by a landslide."

Other approaches may come to mind as you write a story. Use the one that fits the particular situation best.

Time and Tense

Listeners expect broadcast news to be up to date. Without misleading, your writing can make it sound fresh and current even if its's getting a little older than you'd like at times — as in the early morning when most of the file is what happened yesterday. For example, the morning paper says:

President Carter yesterday began a study of...

Continuing tense can freshen it:

President cater is studying...

So can present perfect:

President Carter has begun a study of...

Ask yourself what the current situation is and use the most appropriate tense, which may well be different from the

145

past tense rigidly used by newspapers. Write:

> The Kroger Company announced today that it is (NOT was) closing its stores in Wisconsin.

Commission reports, budgets, and other such documents are like literature in that they are there for the record. So:

> The Commission's report calls (NOT called) the shootings unreasonable, unjustified over-reaction and blames (NOT blamed) them on the police.

Similarly, beliefs and opinions don't normally change overnight. So you're actually being more accurate when you write:

> Mayor Soglin said he thinks (NOT thought) Madison's economic future looks (NOT looked) good.

Using present and continuing tense helps you avoid constantly repeating the words "yesterday" and "today" in the many items which make up a newscast. For the matter, "yesterday" is implied for many stories in the early morning newscast — congress, speeches, news conferences, etc. And on a late afternoon or evening newscast, "today" may be assumed for most of them. so the "yesterday" or "today" does not have to be repeated in every story. The tricky time — when there's likely to be a mixture of today and yesterday stories — is between mid-morning and mid-afternoon. When there's danger of having the listener think a yesterday story happened today, include the time element.

Never use a story that has been out more than 24 hours. It's no longer news. You waste the time of listeners or viewers when your 10 p.m. newscast includes stories they read several hours earlier in the morning paper. This happens quite often where some of the newspersons apparently don't bother to read the morning paper. The wire service rewrites the story from the morning paper and sends it over in present perfect tense. Since all these writers or editors know is what they read on the radio wire, they assume that it is fresh news.

Never assume that a wire story written in present perfect tense (..."has done" such and such...) is a today story. Unless you are absolutely sure, don't change it to past tense

Chapter 13

with the time element (..."did" such and such "today"...). Among other journalistic travesties inflicted upon listeners and viewers are yesterday's stories reported as having happened today.

When "Yesterday" is used, it is sometimes effectively delayed until the second sentence. Example:

President Carter has appealed to members of the United Nations to help in working for peace in the Middle East. He told the General Assembly yesterday...

Do not use both present perfect tense and the time element in the lead sentence. Write either "has said," "said today," or just "said," but not "has said today."

It's yesterday, today, and tomorrow — NOT Monday, Tuesday, and Wednesday.

Never use such time redundancies as 10:30 a.m. this morning or tonight at 7 p.m. Omit the p.m. or a.m. in these cases.

Choosing The Best Word

Contractions judiciously used are an asset in broadcast writing. They're much used in speech and our "ear" copy tends to sound stilted without some of them. Walter Cronkite does not normally sign off with: "And that is the way it is, Tuesday, etc." That's just not the way it's usually said.

But don't overdo contractions. Often, for emphasis or clarity, "not" should be used instead of a contracted form. Unless emphasis of "not" is wanted, "won't" is fine. But you're safer in getting across with "cannot" and "would not" than with "can't" and "wouldn't." The nasal "n't" is easy to lose in enunciation or transmission. Keep that sort of thing in mind — or in ear — as you write.

Avoid cumbersome words when simple ones are available. Why say "approximately one million dollars" when "about one million dollars" does the job as well? There's nothing wrong with "about" used as an adverb. As other examples, simplicity recommends "begin" over "commence," "try" over "endeavor," "buy" over "purchase" and "says" over such often strained and even incorrect synonyms as

147

"declares," "states," "asserts," and "announces." Of course, if the source does indeed make an announcement or issue a statement, then "announced" or "stated" are appropriate.

When should "that" introduce a clause? A good ear is the best guide. "Announced" and "reported" will be followed by "that" more often than will "says" or "said."

In general, when two acceptable forms of a word are available, use the simpler one: "toward" (NOT "towards")... "in regard to" (NOT "in regards to")... and in enumerating "first," "second," and "third" (NOT "firstly," "secondly," and "thirdly."

Television is a medium — NOT a media (plural).

Don't confuse robbing and stealing. A robber takes by force or threat of force. A thief steals — by stealth. DO NOT say that a robber stole 5-thousand dollars from a bank or that a thief robbed a woman of her purse while she was not looking. A robber only robs or takes. A thief only steals.

Watch out for sibilants in succession — the "hiss." Try this one from a UPI stylebook: "Since Senator Sam Simpson has seen Secretary of State Sawyer, he says..." Or the old one Phil Harris used to do: "Six tall slim, slick sycamore saplings..."

Don't abbreviate, except for Mr., Mrs., Ms. and Dr. Spell out: Captain Johnson, Professor Jones, State Street, November 15th, 10 dollars, 15 per cent, etc.

Most stations use Mr. only for members of the clergy. A few use it for the President of the United States.

When you want initials read as such, use hyphens: N-A-A-C-P, R-O-T-C, C-B-S, and U-S. When treating them as a word, omit the hyphens: NATO.

When it's opinion rather than established fact, don't use "pointed out," "noted," or "stressed that." Example:

> The assemblyman said (NOT noted) that out-of-state students are the worst trouble-makers.

Avoid stereotypes, cliches and fad expressions. Such stereotypes as "hippies," "hardhats," "hawks" and "doves" are gross oversimplifications which often do a disservice to the great variety of individuals in the real world. Cliches such as "mounting tension," "massive attacks," and "mute evidence"

Chapter 13

are fairly inocuous, but you can add class to your writing by avoiding them. And most writers do well not to use or (as likely) misuse such "in" (and soon "out") expressions as "right on" or "lost his cool."
Include pronouncers for difficult words which may be unfamiliar to the newscaster. He or she should know Saigon, Haiphong, and Hanoi by now, but could well be misled by Patna (PUTT-nuh), India. And foreign cities to the contrary, it's Cairo (KAY-roe), Illinois, and Versailles (ver-SALES), Kentucky.

Numbers

Treat numbers in the way they'll be most easily and accurately read by the newscaster. Some stations spell out almost all numbers, thus providing a check against typos on the relatively little used upper row of typewriter keys. But spellouts of numbers like 365 can become cumbersome, and many newscasters prefer the numerals. Policies on numbers vary from one newsroom to another and can be confusing. Only a few changes from regular newspaper style are called for.

Round off large numbers when the exact figure is not essential. For example, $54,136 can usually be treated as 54-thousand dollars. Or if you feel it should be made clear that this is not the exact figure — about 54-thousand dollars.

If the number you plan to use ends in two or more ciphers, spell out what the ciphers stand for. For example: 5-hundred, not 500; 8-thousand, not 8,000; 15-million, etc. This keeps the newscaster from having to count ciphers before reading the number. On numbers from thousands up, when something more exact is demanded, do it: 5-thousand 280 or 2-million 400-thousand.

The newspaper's $1.7 million dollars becomes one-point-7 million dollars or one-million 700-thousand, and 1.5 million becomes one and a-half million. (Always write out one when it stands alone.) On some typewriters the numeral "1" is the same as the letter "l."

149

Write dates as you want them read — February 28th, not 28; May 7th, not 7; etc. Don't spell out years — 1972 is fine.

Mechanics

Use normal capitalization. Do not use ALL CAPS in copy the newscaster is to read. They should be reversed for pronouncers and technical cues such as: CART #3 or TAKE FILM.

Use normal punctuation in most cases. Be sure to put commas on both sides of elements in apposition. When you want the appposition to stand out clearly, dashes may be used. Broadcast writers sometimes use three dots instead of a comma between parts of a compound sentence...before a subordinate clause that trails off a sentence ...or between the units of a series when each unit is several words long. But use dots and dashes sparingly, and if in doubt, stick to normal punctuation.

Triple-space. This leaves room for neatly typed corrections.

Don't split words between lines. This can bring an inappropriate pause in the middle of a word.

Use paragraphs logically. If a Viet Nam wrapup story has three distinct aspects, it makes sense to use three paragraphs.

Unless you have a couple of items you're absolutely sure will be used in one-two order, start each story on a separate page. This makes it easier for the editor to shuffle them around and do last-minute updating.

Never hand a newscaster messy or unedited copy. Corrections should be neatly made, preferably typed in above the corrected line. Scribbling and exotic printing are unacceptable. The linotype operator can stop for a while to decipher it, but not the newscaster. If you mess up a word, try again. When you've completed a story, blacken Xed-out portions with a copy pencil. If a page has many corrections and you possibly have time, type it over.

Chapter 13

Voice Reports and Actualities

Voice Reports of correspondents (like Phil Jones of CBS) and actualities which let the listener hear the voices of newsmakers (like Senator McGovern) should add to — not duplicate — what the newscaster says. Especially avoid letting the last words of the newscaster be the first word of the tape.

Bad intro:
> President Weaver said the proposed legislation could ruin the University of Wisconsin.
> WEAVER CART (#8)...TIME — :35
> TAPE OPEN: "The proposed legislation could ruin the University of Wisconsin..."
> OUT CUE: "...the regents and I will stand firm."

Better intro:
> President Weaver commented on the legislation.

Keep lead-ins to voice reports general and brief. Example:
> A new crisis in Jordan. That story from Bob Richards in Amman.

Avoid much redundancy between the newscaster and the correspondent. Broadcast time is too valuable for the newscaster to tell a story and then call in a correspondent to tell the same thing in different words. Sometimes this happens because the writer or editor has not listened to the tapes carefully before incorporating them into the newscast.

After the Weaver actuality and most others, find a way to work in the newsmaker's name again. This serves listeners who missed or only half-caught the name in the introduction and are now wondering who that was. It is usually best handled by telling something else the person said. Example:
> President Weaver said he will talk with the governor on the matter next week.

151

Such tape wrap-arounds, as they are sometimes called, are not necessary if the voice is a very familiar one like President Carter's or Senator Humphrey's or if the actuality is extremely brief — say 15 seconds or less. Nothing further is needed, of course, when a correspondent signs off a voice report with his or her name.

Present tense may be used to introduce a correspondent's voice report — "Phil Jones reports from Washington." But past tense normally should be used for actualities — "Senator Percy explained his opposition." NOT Senator Percy explains..." — lest it mislead by sounding as if Percy is on live instead of taped.

When the correspondent is on tape (as is usually the case), don't write: "We switch..." "We go to..." or "We call in..." This gives the false impression that Phil is on live.

It is professionally dishonest, though perhaps technically correct, to imply exclusivity where it does not exist. For example, a station subscribing to the UPI Audio Service might be technically correct in introducing a UPI Audio voice report: "Pye Chamberlain reports for W--- News." Yes, he's reporting for W--- AND 300 other stations. Even worse, an audio service actuality may be introduced as if it had been acquired through the efforts of the local station. Heard on a Wisconsin station: "Governor Reagan told W--- News." Stations practicing such fraud lower their credibility among the many listeners who can see through it and also invite trouble from the Federal Communications Commission.

Tapes must be clear and understandable if they are to communicate rather than serve largely as a gimmick. If one from overseas transmission is so garbled that it's hard to follow, or if the witness sounds as if she had mud in her mouth, ask yourself — is this really necessary? You do the listeners no service by broadcasting something they cannot understand. That's not communication. And remember, when judging the technical quality of a recording, it's easier to understand in the ideal acoustical setting of the station than on the freeway.

If an engineer is running the tapes, give him or her a carbon of the script with everything he or she needs to know made perfectly clear. This includes the newscaster's introduction, identification of the tape, its exact time, and the closing cue (last words on the tape). Some stations also require the opening cue. And be sure the engineer knows about how far into the newscast the tape comes.

You're Also A Reporter

In most newsrooms, the news writer or editor (often the same person) is also a reporter. Much news can be gathered by phone. If the Wisconsin Automobile Club last night launched a campaign against 65-foot trucks, calls to leaders in the trucking industry may put a new lead on the story you write for the noon news. And if you're writing that police still are looking for a bank robber or that someone remains in critical condition, check police or the hospital shortly before airtime to be sure that such is the situation.

In handling news agency stories, be alert for angles of particular interest to your audience. The list of witnesses called before a congressional committee may include someone from your state. And in the tally of votes for and against a bill, look for how your state's delegation voted.

Although the five Ws and the H should not be crammed into the lead, they are still useful. Before wrapping up a story, ask yourself if all these questions — who? what? where? when? why? how? — pertinent to the story have been answered.

If an important question is not answered by news agency copy or other source material available in the newsroom, you may be able to get on the phone and track down the answer yourself. Such initiative separates the broadcast journalists from the mechanical writers.

Responsibility

Accuracy is highly important in broadcast news. With radio especially, a correction may reach relatively few of the people who heard the newscast on which the error was made. Check out anything that's questionable. For the responsible radio or television journalist, it's more important to get it right than to get it on first.

Don't state cause-and-effect unless you're sure (and you seldom are). Heard on a network newscast:

The campaigning of President Nixon and Vice President Agnew has apparently won several key seats for the Republicans in the Senate.

Maybe so. Maybe not. For all you can prove, the seats were won despite the efforts of Nixon and Agnew.

Controversial matters by definition have two or more sides. Seeking out and reporting all significant points of view is your professional responsibility as a journalist and your legal obligation under the Fairness Doctrine. Because most stories are shorter for broadcast than for print, it's not always easy to include both sides. But if you can find time to report charges against a person or organization, try to find time to seek out and report a reply to them. This is only fairplay.

A note on colorful and "cute" writing. A few "whoop it up" stations have gone off the deep end with over-personalized, over-dramatized news writing. In their efforts to make a show of it, they sometimes distort the news and embarrass persons in the news. When there's doubt as to the accuracy, fairness, or good taste of something imaginative that pops into your mind, skip it. Write interestingly and perhaps on a light story a bit lightly. But for most stories, your best bet is to play it straight. Your primary job is to inform rather than to entertain.

Putting the Newscast Together

In picking a lead story, consider such factors as significance, interest, and immediacy.

Immediacy is usually given higher priority for hourly newscasts than for the longer wrapup news programs. When you're going on with a newscast every hour, a fresh lead story helps keep the overlap listeners from feeling they are getting the same old report hour after hour.

Significance gets higher priority in the longer, more comprehensive wrapup programs. The signoff news on local stations and the early evening network television news programs usually lead with the top story of the day even if it broke in the morning.

Chapter 13

If a good story is an exclusive for your station, or if you have especially good tape or film with it, the story may be given higher priority.
As editor, you can help the listener by lining up the stories so that the newscast has continuity. Some departmentalization is usually desirable. Stories may be grouped by geographic area (world, national, state, and local), by topic area (war, Congress, labor, etc.), or by a combination of the two. Few stations follow the more or less rigid departmentalization prescribed by some of the older textbooks. News value and the pace of the newcast should also be considered. Perhaps your biggest story of the day is local, there are some important world-national stories, and several relatively minor state and local items. You might appropriately organize your newscast in exactly that order.
Sometimes a change of pace is needed in a heavy file of significant but dull news. For example: Congress on the budget, defense spending, and housing legislation; anti-war demonstrations in various parts of the nation; back to Congress on consumer protection and oil depletion allowances.
Transitions can be helpful. If you have school busing stories from Chicago and Birmingham, you might go from one to the other with "In Birmingham..." But use the dateline lead sparingly. And go easy on all transitions. Some have been so overworked that they are best avoided — for example: "On the labor scene..." "Turning to..." and "Meanwhile..." Edwin Newman of NBC News tells of going back to some copy from his early days as a correspondent, striking out every "meanwhile," and finding that not one of the many had been needed.
A simple transition from world to state news is "In Georgia news ..." A more sophisticated transition is none at all, as such. Simply let the opening words of the first state story be something like "The Georgia legislature..."
Wrapped-up stories (those on which no new developments are expected) should normally be written first, leaving the time nearer the newscast for breaking stories. This can cut down on the rewriting and revising you have to do.

155

Handbook for Third World Journalists

A Frame of Mind

The numerous other suggestions which could be included in this broadcast news writing guide would still be aimed at the same two objectives stated at the start: (1) making the news easy for the newscaster to read and (2) making it easy for the listener to understand.

Keeping in mind specific points to help you achieve these objectives can be useful, especially for the beginner. But you'll become a really effective radio or television news writer only when these things blend into a frame of mind which marks your approach to the writing — a constant awareness that this is oral communciation of news. You're writing talk copy.

What goes through your mind as you write a broadcast news story? Possibly something like this. You have the facts, a full two pages of notes or 30 inches of wire copy. But you have time for only 10 lines.

First you decide what is news, what is really important, how you'll use these 10 lines. You know you can include only the essence, so ask — what's the story all about? What has happened that should interest our listeners? What information is most important to pass along to them? The list of names, those little details, some of those figures — no time for them and few listeners would catch them anyway. They would only clutter your copy, detracting from what's really news.

Having decided what's news, you simply tell the listener about it — writing in much the same words and style as if you were telling the highlights to a half-interested stranger, with only 40 seconds to get your message across. The lead sentence should draw attention and let the listener know what the story is all about. Now come the specifics that develop the story, flowing logically and easily from one to the next as in effective conversation. Your story is interesting, informative, and easy to follow. You're talking the news with your typewriter.

Chapter 13

Addendum
CODE OF BROADCAST NEWS ETHICS
RADIO TELEVISION NEWS DIRECTORS ASSOCIATION

The following Code of Broadcast News Ethics for RTNDA was adopted January 2, 1966, and amended October 13, 1973.

The members of the Radio Television News Directors Association agree that their prime responsibility as journalists — and that of the broadcasting industry as the collective sponsor of news broadcasting — is to provide to the public they serve a news service as accurate, full and prompt as human integrity and devotion can devise. To that end, they declare their acceptance of the standards of practice here set forth, and their solemn intent to honor them to the limits of their ability.

ARTICLE ONE

The primary purpose of broadcast journalists — to inform the public of events of importance and appropriate interest in a manner that is accurate and comprehensive — shall override all other purposes.

ARTICLE TWO

Broadcast news presentations shall be designed not only to offer timely and accurate information, but also to present it in the light of relevant circumstances that give it meaning and perspective.

This standard means that news reports, when clarity demands it, will be laid against pertinent factual background; that factors such as race, creed, nationality or prior status will be reported only when they are relevant; that comment or subjective content will be properly identified; and that errors in fact will be promptly acknowledged and corrected.

ARTICLE THREE

Broadcast journalists shall seek to select material for newscasts solely on their evaluation of its merits as news. This standard means that news will be selected on the criteria of significance, community and regional relevance, appropriate human interest, service to defined audiences. It excludes sensationalism or misleading emphasis in any form; subservience to external or "interested" efforts to influence news selection and presentation, whether from within the broadcasting industry or from without. It requires that such terms as "bulletin" and "flash" be used only when the character of the news justifies them; that bombastic or misleading descriptions of newsroom facilities and personnel be rejected, along with undue use of sound and visual effects; and that promotional or publicity material be sharply scrutinized before use and identified by source or otherwise when broadcast.

ARTICLE FOUR

Broadcast journalists shall at all times display humane respect for the dignity, privacy and the well-being of persons with whom the news deals.

ARTICLE FIVE

Broadcast journalists shall govern their personal lives and such nonprofessional associations as may impinge on their professional activities in a manner that will protect them from conflict of interest, real or apparent.

ARTICLE SIX

Broadcast journalists shall seek actively to present all news the knowledge of which will serve the public interest, no matter what selfish, uninformed or corrupt efforts to color it, withhold it or prevent its presentation [by others]. They shall make constant effort to open doors closed to the reporting of public proceedings with tools appropriate to the broadcasting (including cameras and recorders), consistent with the public interest. They acknowledge the journalist's ethic of protection of confidential information and sources, and urge unswerving observation of it except in instances in which it would clearly and unmistakably defy the public interest.

ARTICLE SEVEN

Broadcast journalists recognize the responsibility borne by broadcasting for informed analysis, comment and editorial opinion on public events and issues. They accept the obligation of broadcasters, for the presentation of such matters by individuals whose competence, experience and judgement qualified them for it.

ARTICLE EIGHT

In court, broadcast journalists shall conduct themselves with dignity, whether the court is in or out of session. They shall keep broadcast equipment as unobstrusive and silent as possible. Where court facilities are inadaquate, pool broadcasts should be arranged.

ARTICLE NINE

In reporting matters that are or may be litigated, the journalist shall avoid practices which would tend to interfere with the right of an individual to a fair trial.

ARTICLE TEN

Broadcast journalists shall not misrepresent the source of any broadcast news material.

ARTICLE ELEVEN

Broadcast journalists shall actively censure and seek to prevent violations of these standards, and shall actively encourage their observance by all journalists, whether of the Radio Television News Directors Association or not.

Nigerian Broadcasters try out studio facilities at the School of Journalism, The University of Georgia.

Chapter 14
Putting the Newscast Together
by Vernon A. Stone

One of the truly grand old pioneers of radio news — the late Paul White — used to tell journalism students that putting together a newscast involves the little Red School House formula of readin', 'ritin', and 'rithmetic.

Here's how the formula applies to three basic steps of putting news together into a smooth-flowing continuity of thoughts and details.

1. Readin'... Read all the news copy available, local and wire, and place different stories in different baskets or piles according to your own classification. You may want to use such categories as local, state, regional, national, foreign, Washington, politics, fires, etc. You don't need any fancy filing kit — just stack the stories by classifications which will help you to evaluate the news and decide what to put on the air.

2. 'Rithmetic... You know how much copy you need to fill the airtime. After you decide what stories you're going to use, assign a given number of typed lines to each item so that the total of your cast will exactly fill the available time. Include opening and closings, commercials and station identification.

3. 'Ritin'... Write and edit the news to the number of lines assigned each item. Arrange the items in the order they'll be put on the air. Departmentalize if possible, and write transitions or coupling pins between items where appropriate. Then edit your total cast down to the exact number of lines required to fill the time.

This is a simplified version of what's involved in putting a newscast together. With this mechanical formula, of course, go such intangibles as news judgement, background knowledge, local situation and station policy. But if you follow this basic procedure you'll avoid getting tangled in yards and yards of copy and making hasty last-minute judgements.

Here is an example of how one California editor applied these basic steps in putting together a 10-minute newscast which went on the air at noon.

Editing a 10-Minute Newscast

The editor had before him 3 1/2 hours of local and wire (news agency) news. He knew it was the policy of his station to provide announcers and newscasters with an average of 16 typed lines of copy for each minute on the air. He also knew that opening and closing the news program required 5 lines. So here was the beginning of his 'rithmetic.

10 minutes @ 16 lines each minute...	160 lines
Less opening and closing ...	5 lines
Total for news...	155 lines

With that total 155 lines in mind he read all the available news copy. He piled it according to categories. Then he selected these items for the newscast:

3rd satellite launched ...	national
Queen candidates ...	local
Professor to speak ...	local
Teacher recruitment ...	local
Easter seal drive ...	local
Bus fare cut ...	local
Women's Club Scholarship ...	local
White House on recession ...	national
Astronaut's death ...	national
Confessed slayer ...	national
Gossip screens ...	international
State whips Stanford ...	local
Hockey ...	national
West Coast baseball ...	local
Major league baseball ...	national
Basketball playoffs ...	national
Japanese wrestler ...	local
Championship boxing ...	national

Chapter 14

Timing the Closing Item

The editor then went back to his 'rithmetic. On the basis of experience he knew he would have 5 lines of weather. He regarded that as a must item, last on the newscast.

He next decided the item on gossip screens in England would make a bright "zipper." That would be the next-to-the-last item on his cast so he immediately set aside 5 lines for the zipper and marked it must.

From the 155 lines available for news he subtracted the 10 lines for the zipper and weather. That left him 145 lines for the 17 news items he had selected for the cast. Aiming at the 145 total, and evaluating the news on the basis of his judgement and experience, he assigned to each of the 17 items the following number of lines:

3rd satellite launched ...	national ...	9 lines
Queen candidates ...	local ...	5 lines
Professor to speak ...	local ...	7 lines
Teacher recruitment ...	local ...	7 lines
Easter seal drive ...	local ...	9 lines
Bus fare cut asked ...	local ...	9 lines
Women's Club Scholarship ...	local ...	6 lines
White House on recession ...	national ...	9 lines
Astronaut's death ...	national ...	7 lines
Confessed slayer ...	national ...	6 lines
State whips Stanford ...	local ...	6 lines
Hockey ...	national ...	4 lines
Weat Coast baseball ...	local ...	16 lines
Major league baseball ...	national ...	9 lines
Basketball playoffs ...	national ...	12 lines
Japanese wrestlers ...	local ...	8 lines
Championship boxing ...	national ...	20 lines
Total		149 lines

The editor missed his 145 line objective by 4 lines but he decided to go ahead and write the news according to the 149 line schedule, insert transitions, and then edit the whole cast down to the 145 line maximum.

Then came the 'ritin.' The editor put aside until last the satellite story because the wire service was carrying additional information. The editor, with the assistance of a sports writer, then wrote and edited the various items to the assigned number of lines.

Arranging the Stories

Next came the arranging of the stories. The editor decided the satellite story was the lead — the top story and the latest-breaking story of the day. He could see little departmentalizing other than by local and national categories. So he arranged the cast this way:

3rd satellite launched ...	national
White House on recession ...	national
Astronaut's death ...	national
Confessed slayer ...	national
Professor to speak ...	local
Easter seal drive ...	local
Teacher recruitment ...	local
Bus fare cut asked ...	local
Queen candidates ...	local
Women's Club Scholarship ...	local

Sports

State whips Stanford ...	local
Japanese wrestlers ...	local
West Coast baseball ...	local
Major league baseball ...	national
Hockey ...	national
Basketball playoffs ...	national
Championship boxing ...	national
Zipper ...	humor
Weather ...	local

Inserting Transitions

The editor next read through his cast to decide where transitions could be appropriately used to help move the listener from one story to another. He wrote in 3 lines of transitions.

Chapter 14

More 'rithmetic showed he was now 7 lines over his goal of 145 lines because he had added 3 lines of coupling pins to this 149 budget. He decided to cut to the 145 maximum by editing 7 lines from the 20-line boxing story.

Last-Minute Checks

With most of his newscast ready for the newscaster, the editor telephoned the local weather bureau and wrote 5 lines of weather as previously planned. He added his weather and zipper at the bottom of the cast and was then ready for a last-minute check on the satellite.

He telephoned the San Diego satellite tracking station and was told that station had not yet picked up the 3rd satellite. He tore the lastest satellite news from the ticker and wrote 9 lines, leading with the local angle. His cast was ready for the air.

Just before airtime, the news ticker carried this bulletin — "It has just been announced that the Explorer satellite launched today is in orbit around the earth." The editor handed this bulletin to the newscaster who ad libbed into the cast as a substitute for the language — "The Army has not yet stated whether or not the moon is in orbit."

The Basic Arithmetic

The basic 'rithmetic done by the editor throughout his putting together of the newscast looked like this:

Total for 10 minutes airtime ...	160 lines
Less	
Opening and closing ...	5 lines
Zipper ...	5 lines
Weather ...	5 lines
Total...	15 lines
Left for news items ...	145 lines
Allocated to news items ...	149 lines
Transitions written ...	3 lines
Total ...	152 lines
Cut from boxing story ...	7 lines
Final news total ...	145 lines

Measuring Copy

As the basis for his arithmetic the editor must know how to accurately fit copy to his time limitations. Copy is measured for time by the average number of words to be read in one minute. Most writers and editors arrive at this measurement by counting typed lines.

There seems to be no agreement on the number of words a "typical" newscaster should read in one minute. One large station says its studies show 175 words a minute is ideal. Other stations prefer a count as low as 150. Some newscasters average even more thant 175.

So if you're writing for a radio or TV station follow the policy of that station as to the number of words each minute.

Here's one practical way to fitting copy to time.

Set the typewriter margins at 10 and 75. That setting should give you an average line of 10 words. The newscasters, depending on their own habits, will read an average of 15, 16 or 17 of these lines a minute.

Therefore you can tailor your copy to station policy by simply counting the number of typed lines.

For the purpose of this chapter, station policy will be 16 lines a minute. So you'll need 80 lines for 5 minutes, 160 lines for 10 minutes and 240 lines for 15 minutes. These totals, of course, must include any openings and closings, commercials and station identifications.

This system of fitting copy to airtime isn't foolproof. Some newscasts will include more hard-to-read words than others. Some will include more material to be read slowly for emphasis and understanding. So many stations help the newscaster by 2 other devices, (1) signals from an engineer or editor, and (2) backtiming the last 2 or 3 minutes of the news.

Sign Language

Sign language in radio has become widely used and universal in nature. It's used when the newscaster is before the mike and can't indulge in conversation. By signals, the editor or engineer coaches him.

Chapter 14

The signs below, with slight variations, are used in this mysterious hand waving. If the editor or engineer wishes to relay information to the man at the mike he does it in this form:

Message	Signal
Watch me for cue	Points to one of his eyes with an index finger
You're on the air	Points an index finger directly at newcaster
Slow down	Draws hand apart slowly as though stretching something
Speed up	Points an index finger at the newscaster and rotates hand clockwise rapidly
Everything OK	Forms circle with index finger and thumb, other fingers extended
Two minutes left	holds up 2 fingers
One minute left	Holds up one finger
Half minute left	Makes T with index fingers
You're off the air	Draws as index finger across throat as though cutting it
Move back from mike	Moves hand away from face, palm out
Move closer to mike	Moves hand toward face, palm in
Speak louder	Moves hands up, palms up
Speak softer	Moves hands down, palms down

If the newscaster wants to ask if the program is running according to schedule he touches his nose with an index finger. If the answer is "Yes," the editor or engineer touches his nose. If the answer isn't "Yes," the signalman coaches the newscaster by using the appropriate signal.

Backtiming

"Backtiming" the last 2 or 3 items in a newscast can help the newscaster adjust his pace to avoid noticeable hurry or delay the last minute or so of his program.

Backtiming simply means that an editor actually reads the last 2 or 3 items on the cast against a stopwatch. He marks the required time on each of the backtimed items, then tells the announcer exactly when he should start reading the first backtimed item to finish on schedule.

This backtimed material should be prepared and timed before the remainder of the cast is processed. It should be clipped to the closing remarks — also backtimed — and set aside within ready reach.

Here's how to backtime your cast:

1. Prepare the copy to be timed first. This copy should, if possible, be completed and timed before you write the balance of the cast.

2. Determine the exact time required for this copy by reading it against a stopwatch. Mark this time in the right-hand margin of each item.

3. Include the program closing.

4. At the top of the first page of the backtimed copy write in heavy figures the time of the day at which the newscaster should start reading the copy if he is to finish on schedule.

Simplicity in Makeup

General makeup of a newscast calls for simplicity. It leads with the story of most interest, then follows with less important items arranged if possible in a pattern that has as few jolts as possible between stories. And to keep the listener to the end, makeup saves for last the 2 items with universal appeal — weather and humor.

An ideal newscast contains stories so related and arranged that the listener is moved from one item to another without confusing abruptness. But this ideal condition is rare. News just doesn't seem to break that way.

Chapter 14

Departmentalization and Coupling Pins

So to help the newscaster lead his listeners from subject to subject many editors use 2 devices, (1) departmentalization, (2) transition lines, otherwise known as coupling pins.

Departmentalization — grouping news items by subject or geography — helps the listener evaluate the news and helps the newscast flow smoothly.

Coupling pins — word bridges between items — helps the newscaster lead the listener from one story to another without attention-losing voids or jolts.

Some editors like and use these devices. Others feel they aren't needed. There seems to be general agreement that the longer the cast, the greater is the value (if any) of these devices. Certainly there seems to be little need for them in the one- or two-minute summary.

Departmentlalization

In the longer newscast you as editor will frequently have more than one story dealing with the same subject. These may be from one area or several areas. If you like departmentalization you weave these together into what the listener hears as one integrated story.

For instance, you might have 3 incidents of campus unrest in your own area. If you tie these together with a generalized lead you help the listener realize the significance of campus dissent on his own doorstep.

Or even if the 3 incidents occur in widely separated world communities you can aid the listener by departmentalizing them. He better understands the worldwide meaning of student rebellion.

Just about any kind of news can be departmentalized to advantage in longer summaries — crime, riots, school developments, strikes, accidents, space flight, war. Such departmentalization really gives a sense of depth reporting, helps the listener measure the importance of news.

In the same fashion you may departmentalize your news by geography — local, state, regional, national, international.

By so doing, you lead the listener from area to area without those attention-losing jolts.

There's really no conflict between departmentalizing by subject or geography. Both may be used in the same newscast. If used skillfully, they remove barriers to hearing and understanding.

Allan Jackson's Advice

Allan Jackson writes, edits and reads as many as 15 newscasts weekly for CBS Radio. CBS Radio says of him — "He writes by EAR, that's one reason he has so many listeners."

Mr. Jackson insists radio news must F-L-O-W. He says — "Make your copy F-L-O-W. Don't let it jump all over the place." And he argues this F-L-O-W can be accomplished by writing and newscast organization. Here's some of his advice:

"Hear" copy should F-L-O-W. It must move easily. A story should have a beginning, a middle and a finish. So should the broadcast. Simple? Elemental? Just turn on your set and rather sooner than later you will hear the jumble of "see" copy.

You can do a lot to help the F-L-O-W of your news broadcasts by paying a little attention to the sequence of items. They won't always fall into a pattern and there will be times when you will want to emphasize two or more unrelated items because of their importance. Otherwise, however, you can make your writing chores a whole lot easier if you'll stay in one general area of the news, geographical or topical, until you have finished. Why not, for example, write a general summary of what happened in Congress and then go on to another area, instead of jumping back and forth for no apparent reason. (And we shall ignore the childish dateline approach which has the local broadcaster sounding like an utter ass as he brays such edifying datelines as, "The Capitol," "The House," "Again, the House," "Washington," "The nation's capital," "Once more, Washington.")

There are a couple of pitfalls to avoid in trying to make your copy F-L-O-W. Don't strain for connecting words or phrases. Avoid the obvious, the contrive, the manufactured.

Chapter 14

IF there is a comfortable verbal link, use it if this doesn't jar the sensibilities. The word "meanwhile" does. This poor, once useful little word has been so contorted through three decades of broadcasting that the mere sound of it is enough to send shudders up the backbone. There is nothing you can say with the word "meanwhile" that you can't say better without it because, writing for the ear (remember?), you have an added dimension that is not available to the writer for print — inflection. It's inflection that carries one story into the next and makes it apparent that there is no relation, that a change of locale or tenor is taking place in your report. Inflection can do a lot without being affected. After all, inflection is as important as your vocabulary in everyday conversation. Why shouldn't it be a useful tool in your broadcast work?

Let's maintain a sense of logic and reason in our efforts to keep our copy F-L-0-W-I-N-G. There was the example one Sunday morning of a young broadcaster who went into some detail on the effects of an airline crash and then followed this with the painful connector that "another plane in the news this morning is flying President Eisenhower...."

Watch the consequence of your stories and avoid the unnecessary use of titles. If, for example, you're talking about Nikita Khrushchev in one story you ahould not refer to him as "the Soviet Union's Premier, Nikita Khrushchev" in the story immediately following. And for that matter, if he is a pertinent part of the following story, your copy should F-L-O-W from one to the other. It isn't necessary to end the first before starting the second. To illustrate: I once heard a broadcaster in New York talk about a speech by then Vice President Nixon which was devoted, in large part, to Khrushchev. In the very next story the broadcaster, as though encountering the name for the first time, started off, "The Soviet Union's Premier Nikita Khrushchev has arrived... " This sort of thing is jarring to the listener and disruptive to his comprehension of the news.

The young people who aspire to writing positions in broadcast journalism would do well to bear in mind that their opportunity, first for a job, and then for advancement, will be enhanced by their ability to write — accurately, quickly and interestingly — copy that F-L-O-W into the ears of the

171

Handbook for Third World Journalists

customer — the listener. There will always be a place for the writer who can write.
This ends advice from Mr. Jackson.

Coupling Pins

Coupling pins can be used effectively whether or not copy has been departmentalized. A coupling pin is merely a word bridge between stories. It may be written at the end of one item or the beginning of the next.

Actually the coupling pin is throw-away material. It adds no new facts. It can be tossed away and the facts remain unchanged. Yet when skillfully used it contributes to the continuity of a newscast, gives the listener a feeling he's listening to an integrated presentation of news rather than a set of stories selected at random and shoveled at him without related evaluation.

Coupling pins are controversial in radio and TV news. Editors and newscasters disagree on their effectiveness. At one extreme are some veteran newscasters who won't use any transitions, who insist they can carry the listener along with them by their personality and voice punctuation. At the opposite extreme are editors and newscasters who insist on too many coupling pins with a resultant artificiality.

We feel that coupling pins when used with skill and discrimination do effectively help carry the listener from story to story. But a word of warning — don't use them unless they give a natural effect, don't force them.

Without being aware of it many of us use coupling pins in every day conversation. Before we give the hard facts of what we're telling the other fellow wer're likely to use such expressions as:

By the way
That reminds me
As you'll recall
As a matter of fact
And
But
So much for that
However
Also

Chapter 14

These are spontaneous coupling pins. They come naturally when we change a subject or perhaps add a new thought to an old subject.

Competent newspaper reporters have long used transitions. Many competent radio and TV writers use transitions even more effectively by reason of voice presentation.

Geographical Transitions

Geographical coupling pins can be used to advantage. In early radio news the writer and editor used such transitions by simply datelining stories and reading the datelines, such as Lincoln, Nebraska or Washington, D.C. or Paris, France. Few stations today continue that practice. Most weave the geographical transitions into language that fits more smoothly into announcing.

By writing the location as coupling pin you can help the listener move from area to area more smoothly and with less concentration on his part.

Consider, for instance, a situation where the wire service has given you 3 separate stories of Russian fleet activities in situations important to the United States. You might open with a generalized lead such as this:

"The news tonight stresses activities which might be considered unfriendly to the United States. *In the Mediterranean* Soviet electronic spy ships continue to harass U.S. naval craft on maneuver. *In Canada*, a fisherman has reported he thinks he saw 2 Russian submarines off the Vancouver costs. *And southward in Peru* observers say 3 Soviet undersea boats have been operating just off the coast for several days."

First, you help your listener by departmentalizing your news about the Russian fleet.

And second, you help him understand how widespread are these activities by telling him when you move from place to place, by getting him ready for a shift in locale.

It would be unwise — and probably impossible — to present here a list of coupling pins and to say when to use

173

each. There are too many forms of transition, too many times when a coupling pin would be effective and too many times when the same transition would be ridiculous. The beginner will learn to use coupling pins skillfully only through the experience of analyzing and writing and editing radio and TV copy.

One solid bit of advice is this: don't force yourself into looking for transitions to drop between every item — use them only if the result is a natural flow of language and thought.

Paul White, who helped found and develop CBS radio and television news coverage, used to tell journalism students the organization of a news summary was as important as the writing. He said there could be no rule-of-thumb on the time required to put a newscast together, that a 10-minute cast might require as much as 4 hours of work, a 15-minute summary as much as 6 hours. He always insisted most editors wind up with more copy than they can use and that "There never was a script that couldn't be improved by cutting."

Chapter 14

Addendum
STYLE SHEET

Copy Preparation

1. Type all copy in upper and lower case, on a standard size paper — 8 1/2 x 11 inches.
2. Type on one side of the paper only.
3. Triple space all copy.
4. In upper left-hand corner of each page type:
   Your name.
   One or two word slug line (describing story content).
   Date.
5. Leave top 2 1/2 inches (approximately 14 lines) of first page of each story blank.
6. Leave margins of approximately one inch (12 spaces elite type; 10 spaces pica type) to the left and right of copy on every page.
7. Use phonetic re-spelling each time a word that is difficult to pronounce appears in the copy. Such re-spelling should be enclosed in parentheses immediately following the word. (See Phonetic Re-Spelling.)
8. Never split words or hyphenated phrases from the end of one line to the beginning of the next line.
9. End each page with a paragraph. Never continue a paragraph from one page to another. Never continue a sentence from one page to another.
10. Place individual stories on separate pages — except for roundups, headlines, and closely reated stories. Such stories appearing on the same page should be separate by space bars (-0-). An end mark (*###*) should be placed at the end of each story.
11. Do not staple or fold sheets in any way.
12. Indent paragraphs.

Abbreviations

1. Eliminate the use of most abbreviations in broadcast copy; when in doubt, spell it out.
2. Some widely used abbreviations are permissible:
   Time designations (A.M. and P.M.), but use these sparingly. Instead use such phrases as : this morning, tomorrow night etc.
   Common titles (Mr., Mrs., Ms. and Dr.)
   Certain familiar abbreviations or alphabetical designations that are to be read as such:
   (C-I-O) or (F-B-I, P-T-A, S-O-S)
3. Use the full name of an organization when it is first mentioned in a story, thereafter, use the alphabetical designation.
4. Do not abbreviate: states, countries, months, days of the week, Christmas, Junior, Senior, governmental titles, religious titles, military titles, address designations or books of the Bible.
5. Do not use symbols in lieu of words (& for and, # for number).
6. Always separate the letters used in abbreviations or alphabetical designations with hyphens, when each letter is to be pronounced (I-Q...D-A-R...I-O-U), but run the letters together when they are to be read as a word (NATO).

Capitalization

1. Capitalize freely.
2. Capitalize: all proper names, races, nationalities, sections of the country or world, names of religious denominations and words regarding the Deity, names of political parties and words denoting political affiliation, complete names of associations, organizations, streets, etc.

Chapter 14

Names and Titles
1. Avoid beginning a story with a person's name.
2. Unless a title is unwieldy, it is good to have it precede a person's name.
3. It is not necessary to give the complete name and title of a well-known person in public affairs, if his name is used in newscasts day after day.
4. In first reference to a person, use his complete name. In following references the last name will suffice. And exception to this rule is the President of the United States, who should not be referred to by his last name alone. Instead, say: "President Ford." Women should always carry the prefix Miss, Ms., or Mrs.
5. Omit obscure names or persons and places when they are not essential.
6. Omit middle names or initials unless they are widely recognized as part of the name.

Numbers
1. Use only figures and statistics that are essential.
2. Avoid using lists of numbers.
3. Round off large and detailed numbers where possible.
4. Simplify numbers by such generalizations as: about, almost, approximately, at least, more than, and nearly. Write out one through nine.
5. Use figures for numbers 10 through 999.
6. For numbers over 999, use a hyphenated combination of figure and words, 51-hundred, 10-thousand, 13-million, etc.
7. Always spell out and hyphenate fractions: three-fourths, one-half, two-thirds.
8. In writing time, address, dates, and ordinals, use figures. Use st, rd, and th after figures to be read as ordinals.

177

Handbook for Third World Journalists

9. In telephone numbers and auto license tags, use hyphenated figures.
10. In decimals, spell out decimals marks (5 point 2, instead of 5.2).
11. In amounts of money, do not use $ and ¢ signs. Spell out the marks. (18-dollars and 22 cents).
12. In percentages, do not use the % sign. Spell out the sign. (27 percent).

Punctuation

1. Follow traditional punctuation rules in most instances, but use question marks, quotation marks, colons and semicolons sparingly.
2. Punctuate freely if so doing will assist the announcer to phrase this copy more intelligently.
3. Insert a comma before "and" in listing a series.
4. For oral reading, the dash is useful: to set off names ("The new county commissioner — John Smith — has arrived..."); to set off identifications (Joseph Drake — former mayor — said..."); to set off explantory material (The Jaycees — after having returned with the trophy — marched...). The dash is a double hyphen.
5. Three dots in a row may be used for dramatic effect and to indicate a pause. (He stepped into his car, pressed the starter button, and...a blinding flash...).

Quotations

1. Use direct quotations rather sparingly.
2. Convert most direct quotations into indirect quotations, simplifying and condensing as much as possible, but being careful not to distort the speaker's ideas.
3. Avoid the words "quote," "unquote," and "end quote." Instead, where needed use phrases such as "we quote his exact words," "he said — and we quote him," "he continued," "describing it as," "as he put it," etc.

Chapter 14

4. If you must use a long direct quote, break it up with qualifiers letting the listener know when you are quoting the source directly.
5. Most times it is not necessary to tell the listener when a quote is ended, but this should be done when the following language might confuse the listener.

Time Element

1. Use the present tense freely. When it is obvious to all concerned that the event in question happened in the past use the perfect tense. (John Smith has been captured; instead of, John Smith was captured.)
2. Update all copy. Freshen the approach. Look for the today angle. Do not use the words "last night" or "yesterday" in the lead sentence on most stories.
3. Convey a feeling of immediacy through the use of late-breaking stories and appropriate time references.
4. Unless there is a good reason to the contrary, change all wire copy references to other time zones to the correct hour for the time zone in which the broadcast is given.
5. Observe all release dates scrupulously.

Copy Marking

1. Keep copy editing changes to a minimum. If many changes are required, re-type the material.
2. Make such changes as necessary with a soft black pencil.
3. If a story continues over to another page, draw a heavy arrow at the bottom of the first page.
4. In the upper right corner of each page, write with pencil the number of lines on that page.
5. No type of copyreading marks other than those below should be used in preparing news for the newscaster:

Handbook for Third World Journalists

(a) Material can be completely eliminated;
Examples...

The show is to start ~~xxxxx~~ at 8 this evening.

or

The show is to start promptly at 8 this evening.
~~xxxxx Children~~ will be admitted free.

(b) A misspelled word may be corrected by blacking out the entire word and inserting it correctly spelled. Individual letters may not be blacked out and replaced with the correct spelling.

Example... Governor ~~xxxxx~~ *Smith* is to be the speaker.

(c) Limited changes may be made by blacking out material and inserting new material.

Example... The show is to ~~xxxxx~~ *begin* at 8 this evening.

(d) Limited new material may be inserted.

Example... This show is to *be* at 8 tonight.

6. Circle all material the announcer is not to read, such as slugs, number of lines, page numbers, end marks, etc.

7. After the pages of a newscast have been arrange in order, number each page.

8. At the top of page one write the total number of lines in the cast.

9. Announcers will frequently wish to mark their copy in such a way as to aid delivery. Marks commonly used include underlining for emphasis, slash lines for pauses, time designations for back timing, etc. These should not be included by the writer or editor, but should be added by the newscaster.

Chapter 14

Phonetic Re-Spelling

1. Pronunciation guides should be written in all caps and bracketed into the copy after all hard-to-pronounce proper names.
2. The system of phonetic spelling to be used is based on that used by The Associated Press broadcast wire.
3. The accented syllable should be underlined, and where it is important to indicate secondary stress an apostrophe should follow the syllable.
4. The symbol "OW" is subject to misunderstanding, since it can be pronounced as in "how" or as in "tow." Therefore, it is necessary to handle some pronunciations like this:
    Blough   (RHYMES WITH COW).
5. It will be recognized that approximations are necessar in indicating the pronunciations of some foreign names. It is almost impossible for instance to indicate the nasals common to the French tongue.
6. Examples of correct usage of this system are:
    Guantanamo   (GWAHN-TAH-NAH-MOH)
    Juan Matinez   (WAHN MAHR-TEE-NESS)
    Feisal   (FY-SAL)
7. The followiing symbols will be used:
    AH = a in arm   OW = ow in cow
    A   = a in apple   OO = oo in pool
    EH = ai in air   UH − u in puff
    AY = a in ace   KH = is gutteral
    AW = aw in saw   ZH = g in rough
    E   = e in bed   KK = hard c (cat)
    EE = ee in feel   S   = soft c (certain)
    EW = u in mule   F   = ph (photograph)
    I   = i in tin   G   = for hard g (gang)
    Y   = i in time   J   = for soft g (Geroge)
    OH = o in go
8. Never guess at the pronunciation of a proper name. Check it.

181

Chapter 15
Broadcasting: Serving the Needs of Rural Areas in the Third World
By Al Hester

Broadcasters in developing nations who attempt to serve the needs of their predominantly rural populations have one of the most difficult jobs in mass communications.

This is a conclusion reached by many broadcasters who must deal with the problems — and opportunities — of working with a rural target audience. In discussions with radio journalists and television workers in countries where TV is developed, this investigator has found many reasons for the difficulties these broadcasters encounter.

It takes patience and dedication to operate a broadcasting service which has for one of its major components reaching a rural audience. It is easy to become discouraged because feedback is frequently inadequate from listeners, and frequently there is little money to make improvemens which are obvious to the broadcaster. But these are facts of life which must be dealt with in almost all spheres of governmental service in newly independent nations. The struggle to operate a decent broadcasting system is as difficult as many other governmental tasks in the aftermath of wars or revolution, civil strife and frequent internal instability.

Yet the broadcaster can be assured that his or her task is one of the most important in developmental journalism — the press in the service of the nation. Private broadcasting systems, though relatively few in much of the developing world, also have an active role to play in transmitting messages to rural listeners. Especially in Latin America, there are quite a few privately-owned radio stations. While making profit is the primary motivation for these stations, in most countries in the developing world they must be conscious of serving the national needs as well as running a successful business in the broadcast sector. Let it be said that it is not an impossible task for private sector stations to make a real contribution to rural needs, if the station ownership understands the importance of these listeners.

Purposes of This Article

This article proposes to outline some of the problems faced by broadcasters dealing with rural audiences, to give some examples of interesting work being done in several different Third World countries, and to discuss briefly training needs of broadcasters serving domestic audiences, with an emphasis on service to agricultural areas.

Most of the countries in the Third World face these challenges. One of the greatest problems is obsolete and poorly operating equipment. It is not uncommon for many Third World broadcasting stations to be off the air for fairly long periods of tme because of transmitter or other equipment difficulties. Many transmitters — even of national radio services — are 20 to 30 years old. If they are able to transmit, frequently it is at reduced power at only a fraction of the rating wattage. This erratic broadcasting transmission operation reduces confidence in the station, and leaves audiences critical of its performance.

Frequently, too, there is an almost complete lack of necessary recording equipment, studio equipment, good microphones, etc. But the Third World broadcaster is, above all, a pragmatic, make-do, worker. This investigator has even heard of a case where the transmitting antenna was blown down by a hurricane. The low-power broadcaster ran a random-length wire to a palm tree from the transmitter and kept on the air. And surprisingly the signal reached most of the previously reached listening area!

Developed nation broadcasters would be amazed at the primitive equipment which is used in many countries. But somehow the messages go out over the airwaves, although in erratic or sub-standard forms.

Irregular Power Supplies

In many areas, there is no assured power supply, and fluctuations in the mains are the norm, rather than the

Chapter 15

exception. A standby generator is a necessity for almost all stations, if they can afford one.

Another problem is lack of responsible employees who run equipment or act as its custodians. For example, a few years ago, the employee charged with overseeing the ground station linking a portion of Papua, New Guinea, to the satellite network, disappeared, leaving the station unmanned for several days. During that time the satellite linkup was impossible. He had gone up into his mountain village to be married. Along with lack of responsible technicians is the lack of maintenance of equipment. This problem is made much worse by severe environments of dampness and heat which are prevalent in much of the tropical world. And there are the unexpected hazards — one broadcaster going on the air to give a weather report found a rattlesnake coiled around the microphone he was to use.

Another severe problem for many Third World broadcasters is the lack of training of personnel. It is fairly rare for broadcasters to have received formal training in many developing countries. All too commonly, those in radio and television have had to learn on-the-job, feeling it a victory if a signal goes out from the transmitter — never mind the quality of the news or entertainment given over the air. Untrained broadcasters are an even greater problem when it comes to the management of the operation. If the director of broadcasting is untrained, he or she cannot do the necessary planning to run an efficient operation. And the staff frequently has little respect for an untrained director. They look to this official to bring order to an unstable and difficult situation.

But an even more serious problem than lack of equipment, good maintenance and trained employees is the lack of social and political direction of a broadcasting station or system. It is all too obvious that in many nations it has been decreed there will be a national broadcasting system. No concerted communications policy has been developed for any of the mass media. The lack of such a policy and of fitting the media into the social and political environment is even more painfully obvious in broadcasting. Most of the citizenry in many nations are illiterate and pay scant attention to newspapers and magazines. But they all are quick to spot deficiencies in radio and television services. Frequently broadcasters become the butt of jokes by many listeners or viewers who have little idea of the difficulty of broadcasting without direction and with little equipment and expertise. Associated with lack of direction is poor direction from political leadership. It is probably safe to say that political leadership, both national and local, is most jealous of broadcast facilities. Politicians know the power they possess through access to radio and television. Usually the broadcasting station is the first place seized in a coup or change of power. Because these leaders are so sensitive to the power they can exert through broadcasting, they frequently require a hand in setting policies of the station. This is of course to be expected. But the broadcaster is in a difficult situation where political leadership demands run counter to good journalism reflected in dissemination of accurate information and fairness in setting the news agenda. The wise political leader realizes that if he or she requires lies to be broadcast over and over, the population will come to laugh at the broadcasting operation, giving little credence to what is said over the air. In the longrun, it is better to tell the truth and to give a well-rounded picture of reality. This may be painful, but citizens are not stupid. They quickly spot the unethical politician and the supine broadcaster as the lackey of power.

    A case in point recently in Africa has been the refusal of some leadership to deal with the devastating epidemic of AIDS disease. Denying that it exists will not make the problem go away. Yet media workers have been handicapped by political decisions to ignore the problem and forewarn the population. Fortunately the World Health Organization and some national governments are beginning to cope with this question.

    But, all-in-all, the most difficult problem broadcasters face comes from the political environment. A nation's broadcasting system leadership should be high enough up in the power structure to have input into political policies. The use of broadcasting for telling the government's story is necessary in many countries. But it should not be perverted to selfish and corrupted ends of persons in power.

Dealing with Political Leaders

Only a fool goes against the current of power. Survival is necessary first of all. But in many countries, there are ways and ways to work with the political structure. Except in the most rigid authoritarian systems, there is some flexibility and choice to be had in the way the mass media operate.

For instance, it is frequently possible to persuade leadership that a certain course of action is to their advantage (and it often is). If ideas are presented adroitly, without threatening those in power, they may come to see such ideas as their own. Some broadcasters have had fair luck in presenting critical programming, addressing a national problem by not trying to assign blame for it to the current political leadership. Many problems are inherent in the social and political structure dating from colonial times. It is possible to address the problem without pointing the finger of blame.

Sometimes, too, it is possible in a documentary to discuss a major problem, but in a framework of another neighboring country. Frequently the same problems are shared. Listeners and viewers can make the necessary extrapolations to the local situation without it being exactly spelled out. This oblique approach is not the most satisfactory, but half of a loaf is better than none at all.

Some Other Problems

Some other problems which especially affect broadcasting to non-urban areas include the difficulty of the signal reaching these audiences. Many countries have mountainous terrains which frustrate good reception. Others have very scattered populations at considerable distance from the transmitting stations. Other nations are made up of separated parts, such as Indonesia, which has many islands over a very large area.

These problems are met in a variety of ways — if they are met at all. Papua, New Guinea, must cope with very isolated villages surrounded by high mountains. A system of regional and district high-frequency (tropical band) stations has been set up to get signals into these areas. The relaying of signals via communications satellite is being used quite effectively in numbers of countries where terrain makes traditional reception difficult.

A recent rural communications project using the satellite to reach remote jungle areas is in Peru. Peru has a national policy of developing this interior area, and eventually it will produce many food products as settlement increases. The Peruvian National Telecommunications Company and the United States Agency for International Development have joined in this project which links much of the backcountry with Lima and other areas. It will focus upon telephone communication, but more and more broadcast systems are utilizing satellite relays to overcome terrain, distance and interference problems. Many nations now have access to their own satellite, a regional satellite, or space on Intelsat or other internationally operating communications satellites. Costs of access to satellites continue to come down.

The cost of telephonic linkage via satellite or radio signal relaying is quite low, compared with the costs of necessary frequency widths for television transmissions.

Much of the Third World depends upon tropical broadcast band transmissions to link remote areas. While serving this purpose fairly well, such tropical band broadcasts are often subject to thunderstorm interference and vagaries of the ionosphere and the sunspot cycle. Some nations have utilized numerous FM broadcast stations as an alternative, although this proves to be expensive. Better fidelity broadcasts and interference-free transmissions are easier via FM than by the traditional AM transmissions on standard broadcast bands or HF bands.

Ignorance of Target Audiences

One of the most common problems facing broadcasters to rural areas is ignorance of the broadcaster concerning characteristics of the target audience. The broadcaster is told

Chapter 15

to reach the rural areas, but no research is done concerning the likes, dislikes, needs etc., of the agricultural population.

Developed nation researchers frequently criticize this lack of knowledge of the rural broadcaster toward his or her target audience. But criticism is easy. Finding out the needs and desires of a diffuse, scattered and ill-educated population is very difficult. Even with modern sample survey techniques, many rural dwellers are suspicious of people taking information from them.

And this is natural, considering that most of the time government people come to the villager to get tax money out of him or to force him to do something he doesn't want to do. Suspicions must be overcome by poll-takers if they are to be trusted by rural residents. It does little good to send a college graduate from an urban area into remote rural areas and expect him to get valid survey information.

Rural dwellers are also very quick to pick up any condescension evidenced by broadcasting survey people. Too many of the better-educated government employees look down on the poorly educated rural population. They confuse a lack of formal education with stupidity. Yet frequently, farmers or herders are very intelligent. They have had to be, in order to survive drought, disease, poverty and neglect by the central government.

On some broadcastng staffs, an elitist attitude isolates the staff from the audience. The city man's ideas of what is good for the rural listener sometimes are wrong. Get some farmers to tell you what they need.

Of course, another problem faced by those broadcasting to rural areas includes the difficulty listeners may have in enunciating what they want and need from the broadcast programming. They have had no model to hold up before them, so it is difficult for them to envision anything other than what they know. This is where well-trained broadcasting personnel have a responsibility. They must balance what they get from listeners as to needs with intelligent and innovative program efforts which break new ground. Sometimes the only way to find out is to try and then measure the results through surveys, interviews, letters and requests to the station, etc.

Changing Old Habits

Frequently broadcasters are given the job of persuading farmers to adapt new ways of agriculture or living. It has usually been found that merely "preaching the message of change" via the mass media is not enough to persuade farmers to change their habits and to plant new varieties of crops, to practice better sanitation, or to listen to advice.

Radio or television by themselves can't do the job of persuading people to change opinions, habits, etc. A combination of easy-to-understand information plus a chance for listeners to discuss it, argue about it, and make decisions in a personal setting is necessary.

India, for example, has used radio forum groups where the rural listeners get the basic information from radio or television, then have village discussions among themselves and with agricultural specialists who can be of help to them. Frequently broadcasters consider the refusal of rural listeners to change farming practices, habits, etc., at the drop of a hat as mere stubbornness. A farmer or herder must weigh and measure very carefully. He frequently has little or no margin of error. If he decides to plant a new variety of pasture grass, he has to be sure that it will yield at least as much as the old variety. No one will feed his cattle if he makes a mistake.

And in some cultures, farmers are slow to adapt innovations which set them apart from the rest of their friends and neighbors. To be better off than one's neighbors can be dangerous. There is jealousy and envy of the man who succeeds where others fail. The wise farmer knows this. Also, in some societies there is the idea of "divisible good." This means there is only so much good fortune to be had. If you get rich, someone else must get poor to make up for it. If your crops grow where others fail, you are using up the "good" and others will suffer for it. This philosophy sometimes makes rural dwellers slow to adapt new ways. They know they must continue to live in their village and face others who have not made the changes or been so fortunate.

Some rural broadcasting programs have been effective, too, in persuading farmers to take part on-the-air in "talk shows" or "panels" where they discuss their needs and

Chapter 15

problems. Many conservative rural dwellers are reluctant to do this, and patience is needed to get such a program together, but frequently listenership to such program is high. Patient work by radio staffers with panelists is needed to overcome timidity.

In some countries, there is a need to use radio broadcasting for personal messages in rural areas. Where such uses are made, listeners develop a close identification with the station, and the radio becomes indispensable to them. Guatemala, for example, has several stations which specialize in relaying messages from rural areas to city relatives and vice versa. Festivals, birthday celebrations, illnesses and deaths also are announced over the air. Truly such stations become "newspapers of the air." Such stations are then also able to program messages for rural change and innovation because they have become the friend of the the people.

Now that television is in the ascendancy in many countries over radio, some of radio's inherent qualities are being ignored. It is possible for radio to be used to produce documentaries with appropriate dramatic devices, music and good radio acting to present messages with entertainment and social values. In many countries rural programming is only a small fraction of the total broadcast package, often less than 10% of the total. An expanding area might be in documentaries prepared to address a specific problem. For instance, one station broadcast a documentary concerning the effects of tropical rain forest land being cleared in Guatemala to make way for raising more beef cattle. These cattle were then sold to a North American "fast food " company to make into millions of hamburgers. The short-term effect of clearing the forest land was to put money into the pockets of land-owners. But after two or three years, the soil was leached out, fit for nothing at all, impoverishing the areas even further. The documentary produced pointed to these dangers. It is sad to say that a U.S. broadcasting group produced it rather than a Guatemalan broadcaster. But the local stations could have done it — if the political environment allowed.

Imagination and familiarity with rural areas is needed to make such documentaries.

191

Training Efforts

In talking with station directors or other broadcasting officials in developing countries, no areas received more discussion than the need for training. As is true with other mass media, personnel frequently have had little formal training.

A recent trend, however, has been for foreign governments or organizations to offer overseas training for broadcasters. Sometimes this has worked out quite favorably, but there are pitfalls to be avoided. Fairly frequently training offered by organizations outside the broadcaster's country do not make learning relevant to Third World situations. The broadcaster who comes from an ill-equipped station is suddenly bedazzled by an array of expensive and advanced equipment he or she probably won't ever see at home. This leads to frustrations when the employee returns. He or she has been spoiled by programs with more resources than his or her station is likely to have.

Another serious problem for stations sending personnel overseas (even if financial support is donated) is that the long-term absence of key staffers makes the work more difficult for those who remain. And one final difficulty in some overseas training programs is that teaching personnel do not have empathy in dealing with broadcasters from developing nations. Some tend to be elitist or impatient when the broadcaster asks basic questions.

There is a Chinese proverb which says: "He who asks a dumb question is a fool for a minute. He who never asks at all is a fool forever." Educators would do well to keep this in mind and to be patient with questions which are of a basic nature.

Problems of Imitation

Sometimes, too, trainees are beguiled into imitating foreign broadcasting models which have little relevance to a developing nation. Slavish imitation of foreign communication systems hurts the individuality of sovereign nations.

Chapter 15

There are some foreign training programs which are of a practical nature, taking into consideration the needs of the African, Latin American or Asian broadcaster. The Center for International Mass Communication Training and Research of the School of Journalism, University of Georgia, U.S.A., operates out of an academic setting but features instructors with solid media experience. It is able to plan a custom-designed program to meet specific training situations. These programs are not academic credit programs but are certificated adult education programs for career media personnel. They are tailored to keep in mind constraints in cost and time.

Sometimes the Center's programs are taught by a team of two or three instructors who come to the country where in-service training is requested. This is often cheaper than bringing trainees to the United States. The training team works with local equipment and tries to fit in training so that it does not disrupt broadcasting operations, as absences of key personnel tend to do. Typical intensive workshops emphasizing basic instruction last from one week to a few months.

The Center works with governmental organizations, private foundations, professional organizations, worker's unions and journalism groups.

There are quite a few solid regional broadcasting training organizations, and several organizations in the United States and United Kingdom, especially, are happy to work with broadcasters from developing areas.

Patterns of Thinking

Perhaps one of the most important areas for education of broadcasting staff is not so much in the technical mastery of equipment. This is certainly important, but more fundamental lacks must frequently be addressed. These include improving basic reporting skills, sharpening abilities to obtain information, how to do proper interviews and how to get ideas or innovative programming. These do not require high-cost technology.

Salleh Hassan, writing in *Gazette, the International Journal of Mass Communication Research*, in 1986 discussed training problems of Asian broadcasters. Types of training he listed included pre-service training to improve professionalism of existing staff, on-the-job apprenticeships and academic training.

Hassan notes that in-service training is especially effective and that it should accomplish the following tasks:

1. To stimulate open-mindedness and to inhibit poor habits.
2. To provide a constructive rest or sabbatical for employees.
3. To encourage new ideas and update old skills.
4. To encourage the attitude that broadcasting is an organic, changing and demanding profession.
5. To provide opportunity for constructive self-criticism.
6. To show new broadcasters that they don't "know it all."
7. To give feedback from those receiving training to lower levels of employees.
8. To give a continuing source of contact with other professionals.
9. To introduce new techniques and equipment, but to do it where learning faults will not appear public.
10. To provide a forum for professional discussion.

It should be added that a good training program should increase the self-assurance and morale of the broadcaster involved.

A Postscript

Finally, we need to close by relating the whole discussion once again to the end consumer of the messages broadcast — the rural listener or viewer. Any programming done for this group should be cognizant of a special rural environment. Rural Nigeria is not Lagos, nor is rural Mexico the teeming capital, Mexico City.

Broadcasters should realize there is often a very basic conflict in lifestyle and philosophies between rural dwellers and those dwelling in metropolitan areas. Customs are often more conservative in rural aras. Programming which offends moral values of rural listeners does more harm than good. But this does not mean that programs cannot investigate problems caused by the clash of cultures or customs between urban and rural living. Some of the most popular "telenovelas" in Latin America, for example, take for a main theme the rural citizen who must adjust to the urban environment, adopting "modern" ways. A sensitive portrayal of choice involved may be of service to the listener or viewer.

Perhaps one of the most valuable bits of content in the mass media might be to warn rural people that migrating to the huge cities will not necessarily make their lives better or happier. Several broadcasting organizations have treated this theme of rising frustration of rural people who think the city will be Paradise. Such programming may be effective in making at least some rural dwellers think twice before joining the throngs of unemployed and unhoused in overcrowded urban areas.

As the programming officer hunts for ideas with his or her staff, it should not be forgotten that women often are involved as radio or TV listeners, sometimes much more than men. Programming which ignores the needs of women to be more than child-bearers and housekeepers is missing the mark. Many young women working in broadcasting have good ideas about how the media should treat the changing roles of women in Third World countries. Women are beginning, in some countries, to take positions of leadership and to have influence on media content, with the special consideration of women's needs.

The station broadcasting to rural areas must also keep in mind that rural residents of necessity must pay attention to times of reaping and times of sowing. Program schedules may need changing with the agricultural season, or with special festivals and holidays. You ignore these things at your peril. Broadcasters must also keep in mind the fact that not every family will have a radio, and certainly not a TV. They must go to village leaders' or friend's houses. And bad weather may affect their ability to get to radio or TV sets.

Chapter 16

Government-Press Relations in the Third World

By An Anonymous Information Ministry Official

(EDITOR'S NOTE: This high official in the information ministry of a Third World nation requested that he remain anonymous. We think the importance of what he says warrants the publication of his thoughts, although we must do so without identifying him.)

The fact that I must remain unidentified points out the continued stress between government on the one hand and the press on the other. It is an unfortunate truth that in many Third World nations there is very little freedom of expression. Many arguments can be advanced for this situation, and I certainly have sympathy for those who say that an unfettered and uncontrolled press can be a real danger to the survival of the nation. But I must quickly add that in the long-term, the interests of good government and a stable nation are better served by an open communication policy.

Many leaders of the world's nations — and some of these nations are in the developed world as well as the undeveloped countries — sincerely believe that the role of the press is to support unconditionally and with complete enthusiasm whatever the government proposes. They see the press as an integral extension of the central government. Such top leaders believe they have a mandate to rule without having any responsibility to a bunch of semi literate press sensationalists whose intrinsic nature is to make trouble for everybody.

Other leaders I have known sincerely feel that only a handful of government officials and other highly placed members of their society really have enough enlightenment to lead the nation. I call this philosophy "benevolent elitism," and it is fairly common in some countries. These leaders reason that a largely untrained press and a mostly illiterate population can only combine to make the path to a stable nation more difficult. They feel that they have been chosen by the electorate or in other ways — maybe by God — to lead the nation toward independence and happiness.

A few leaders would gladly give more opportunity for a diversified press, if only the infra-structure were present in their country to attract it. But they are perforce required to support what press there is as a part of the government. Their countries are too poor, too illiterate, or too small or isolated to attract press operations by a profit-making group.

I have also had many dealings with certain national leaders who vehemently believe, after looking at the Western press models, that the mass media of the West are nothing more than mongers of materialism and consumerism, only hastening any nation they infiltrate to the loss of national soul and identity. Hence they make every effort to keep out the commercialized mass media from outside their borders. They see no empathy on the part of these money-makers for new nations struggling for their place in the world.

I have met a few leaders who also believe that the Socialist nations export a dull and often untruthful picture of the world through their media systems. Marxists are as anxious to usurp other nations' sovereignty as are some of the capitalists. In the tired tug-of war between capitalism and Communism, the Third World is the battle ground. And it often gets trampled underfoot by East and West.

And finally I have sometimes come into contact with national or regional leaders who don't give a damn about the welfare of anyone but themselves. Their eyes glint with pleasure and anticipation of further enriching themselves at the public expense. And they see any opposition by the press as something to be stepped on, as one does an ugly cockroach on the floor. The press in such countries as these men control is only a trite recitation of the false virtues of the Maximum Leader. The arrogance of such leaders must be disguised as benevolence and caring, when in effect such leaders are as amoral as tom-cats.

Against such a varied background as these concepts of the role of the press in a nation, what can we say? The role of communication and information is a puzzlement to many leaders. Most of the time they have no professional or

Chapter 16

academic background which would help them deal with the problems of communication within a nation. They, with the help of ministry officials, can set up some semblance of a communication system. But too often it is inefficient because of untrained and unmotivated government ministry employees. Too often, running the nation's communications and information set-up is left to fearful subordinates who have come to the practical conclusion that it is better to do nothing than to do something which calls attention to them. Too much attention can be painful, especially if one makes mistakes. While the mistakes of other ministries are sometimes not immediately visible, the mistakes of the infomation ministry are all too evident. Not only the leader sees such mistakes, but so do many of the people in the country. This accounts for a rather high turnover in the information ministries of many countries. Being an information minister is a risky and stress-laden occupation.

Assuming that the information minister or official has the good of his people in mind, there are a few things which may be done toward this end. Rome was not built in a day, nor will an efficient and open communication systen be built quickly and without pain.

The first thing a high information official must do is to search his heart and try to determine honestly if there is any way in which he can be a part of the governmental process. If he reaches the conclusion that the nation's rulers are too corrupt, evil or selfish to allow for any freedom in the land, he is better off digging ground-nuts or fishing somewhere in his little boat. For if he serves a master who deserves an honored place in the Italian Poet Dante's Hell, his life will become a tedious falsehood. He will see little-by-little his ideals worn down, his ethics sucked of their blood, and his personal integrity become as an empty gourd that rattles in the wind.

If, however, he can see the nation's leaders as men who have some good intentions and who have some desire for the betterment of their countrymen, he may decide to stay on duty. He may even entertain hope that he may help bring information to the nation which will be of utility. He may even dream that someday his nation will achieve greatness or that its glories and happiness of ancient days gone by can be restored once again. Such dreams keep men young and make up for the hundreds of battles losts and frustrations suffered. Fortunately many leaders are like the rest of the us. They are just human and are mixtures of good and bad, but not cruel or evil people.

The information official should serve as a bridge between the government and the people. Bridges let traffic cross two ways. The information offical should show that it is just as important to carry information to the top leaders as it is to send it from them to the people. The saddest cases of all among our leaders are those who isolate themselves from the real world of their people. As they gain power, they forget their origins and their responsibilities. Even well-intentioned leaders become isolated, sometimes through just having too much to do. To lead is to be killed — sometimes by enemies but sometimes by the sheer staggering fatigue of dealing with your country's problems. Nothing works. There is no money. There is no trained cadre of officials. Nature has frowned by causing typhoons or droughts. Sometimes these leaders feel as if there is no God in the world, and that they are alone. The wise leader must never lose his knowledge of what goes on outside the wall of the palace. The good information official has a duty to inform those on high as well as those who sweat for their daily bread.

A public information official must first of all try to persuade his bosses and associates that there is something to be gained by being truthful. This is a tremendously difficult lesson to absorb. To admit that we are human, that we on occasion fail, or that the nation is in trouble is hard to do. It takes a man who is at peace within himself, a man who knows that governments change, that the seasons come and go, and that he will in a relatively short time be gone from the scene of this world. One of thr most satisfying things to cherish toward the end of one's life is the feeling of being true to self, to have had integrity and to have run the race honestly to its end. Lies may seem to help for the moment, but in the end as they are placed one upon another, they become a greater and greater burden to maintain, until finally the effort to misinform becomes tremendously costly. Government leaders in the so-called advanced nations have just as difficult a time learning

Chapter 16

this as do Third World leaders. Actually, perhaps a Third World leader can be more easily forgiven for trying to make shift with a pack of lies than can the man who can marshal much resources and talents to governing.

The worst of it is that when the leaders lie to the people, they at some point come to believe their own disinformation. Their governance becomes more and more surrealistic until it bears little resemblance to the real world. Many of us have felt that strange feeling of moving as if through some kind of horrid dream where day follows day in unreality as a nation sinks deeper and deeper into the morass resulting from out-of-touch leadership. Then one day, the sleep is ended — but mostly by a fantastic outpouring of rebellion and revolution. If we communicate truthfully, we can frequently head off such explosions.

The information ministry official must be down-to-earth in his expectations. Caught as he is between his boss and the media or the people of the country, he must recognize his limitation. But if he can reach the top leadership with ideas which improve the the flow of information and bring the nation together, he has done much. At the same time, he can feel satisfaction if he oversees a government information program which brings truthful and interesting information of use to ordinary people. He may do this directly through government communication organs or through the press of his nation if it is separate from government.

The wise information official tries to inform himself about the major communication needs of his country. What do his people need to know? Do they need more information about health measures and how to be better farmers? Do they need to know that there will never be enough jobs in the country if they continue having too many children for the economy to support? Do they need to know that inter-tribal hatreds serve no one well? Do they need to have information to protect themselves against being manipulated by foreign interests set on only their selfish ends?

Do the information official's countrymen need to know how to cope with urban living after migrating to the capital city? Do they need to know the basics of representative government if the country has it, or hopes to have it? Do they need to know how to read and write? After those who set information policy decide what are the major questions to be asked (and to try to answer) for their people, they must come up with ways and means.

Any kind of a policy on the use of communications must consider how training of personnel will be carried out, what resources can be used for this, and what equipment will be needed. The wise information officer is not beguiled mindlessly by the dazzle of high-technology equipment. He will listen carefully and study what mode of communication may be best for the job at hand. Perhaps labor-saving devices are not best. Maybe bicycle deliverymen are better to carry telegrams from the telegraphy office to the recipient than a mass of facsimile printers and computers.

The cautious information official will weigh carefully the problems of emulating a foreign press system just because it offers training, or because he himself has been trained in it. Each country is different. It is vital to take what is of utility and to reject what is not. The information officer must ask himself what mass media operations method or content is counter-productive. He must be able to ascertain WHY anyone wants to operate the mass media in his country. What are their motives? Do they have a stake in furthering national development? Or do they just desire to make money as quickly as possible with no impediments to this process?

When he deals with the press (if there is a separate press in the country), the information official must not lie. He will lose any effectiveness if he misinforms the media. It is better to keep his mouth shut than to tell false stories. He should have some sensitivity to the difficulties of reporters and editors who have little training. They will oftentimes make mistakes. Some of these mistakes will have painful effects upon the government or others. But they must be allowed to learn. If they are kept muzzled, they will never learn to speak. The information official should encourage further training of reporters, editors, cameramen, etc., so that they can become more professional and more ethical. He should encourage employers to pay a decent wage to them.

Chapter 16

A good information official will not slight his own country's reporters in order to give the highly placed foreign journalist an exclusive article. This pandering to the foreigner greatly irritates the local press.

The information officer must also critically examine his own competence to be in communications. Has he had the necessary training? Or was he just a political appointment with no background? If he does not have background in the information business, he had better obtain it, one way or another.

Finally, the information officer, as he looks at government-press relations, should try to keep a sense of proportion. The sun will rise tomorrow and life will somehow go on — even if he makes the wrong decision. He cannot carry the weight of the world on his shoulders. He will fall to the ground under it. And at least once a day, he should laugh — at himself or his follies and foibles, and at the supreme conceit: that what he does will have much impact upon the world as it will be 50 years from now.

Handbook for Third World Journalists

Chapter 17
Education and Training
For Third World Journalists
By Al Hester

The scene: Vienna, Austria, a few years ago.
The event: The meeting of OPEC ministers from some of the richest oil-producing nations of the world.
The characters: The world-wise, suave oil minister of an Arab country. A frightened, inexperienced reporter for an Arab news agency.

Oil Minister: Well, you did show initiative in tracking me down, and for that I'm willing to give you an interview — and because you are from _____ country. What do you have to ask me?

Young reporter: (flustered, confused and with hands shaking) Your excellency....uh, uh, how do you think things are going?

Oil Minister: Can't you be more specific? I'll give you 20 minutes — that is, if you can ask me some intelligent questions.

Fortunately the oil minister, who did have some understanding of the young reporter's problems, went on to toss him a few bones of information for his story. But the reporter later said he was so nervous because of his lack of experience and training that he could scarcely get through the interview.

"I made a vow that I would never be so ill-prepared or lacking in being a good reporter," he told this writer. "And then I spent two years persuading my bosses to let me get some real training for journalism."

The situation of this young reporter was not at all unusual. Hundreds of reporters in the Third World could easily share his shame and frustration at being placed in a situation for which he had little training or education. Events have moved so fast in many Third World countries that reporters often have to assume heavy responsibilities in journalism before they are adequately trained for them. If they are lucky, they learn on-the-job. Or perhaps they have superiors who see the need for additional training and facilitate such training.

Young countries frequently have young educational systems. Poor countries often have few training facilities. It's a safe guess that the majority of journalists in Third World nations feel strongly they should have more training and education. This writer has noticed time after time that one of the first questions asked him as a journalism teacher is, "How can I become better trained, and where should I go to get that training?" This is a serious question. Many Third World journalists see the need for more training to better serve their countries and to make their career more satisfying personally. A good education and training program often is the key to advancement in journalism or in government work.

We are seeing more and more frequently that journalistic training and education is not being left to apprenticeship or cadet programs offered by the various mass media. While life on a newspaper is a quick teacher, it is often painful and the readers (and possibly the paper itself) sometime suffer during the learning process. Lessons learned may be quite agonizing and what training exists is given helter-skelter. Few editors or other reporters are trained teachers and don't have enough time to be very helpful to young reporters, even if they desire to be.

Most countries now have at least one institution for training of their own journalists. And there are many opportunities for training in journalism outside the reporter's own country. The young reporter or the reporter who wishes to improve his or her skills at mid-career must weigh carefully what the possibilities for further training and education are. Most have to settle for what they can get as cheaply and quickly as possible. Some governments will help pay expenses and will be supportive in getting leaves for the reporter to return to school or to the training institution. There are some free programs, too, if the recipient can qualify for them.

Chapter 17

The reporter should first investigate what training is available at-hand in his or her own country. It is not enough to know that a school for journalistic training exists in your country. You need to know the specifics such as what can you study, what facilities are available and how qualified are instructors. The reporter who desires meaningful help in doing a better job will not settle for a scrap of paper which says he is a graduate of a training program, if the program doesn't mean anything. In a small country it is easy to find out how well the the journalist's training school works. You can talk to graduates of the program. You can see how reporters who have trained there perform on their jobs. It is fairly easy to check out the credentials of teachers to see if they ever made their living working in the mass media and how well they write or teach.

If you have evidence that the local or national training program is a good one, it is probably to your advantage to enroll in it. This is frequently quicker and less expensive. But if you have good reason to believe that the training is cursory or inadequately supported in your country, it may be time to shop for better possibilities.

You should be cautious about any program which seems to emphasize too many theoretical courses and too many broad general courses. If you are to become a better reporter, you need a program in which you do a lot of writing, some of it on deadline. You need a program which teaches you how to take notes, how to do thorough interviews, how to think up ideas for worthwhile stories and how to be ethical in your career. Of course, all reporters need education in literature, philosophy, history, politics, history and economics. But these are areas in which traditional colleges frequently have extensive offerings. Journalistic training speaks to the task directly at hand. The good reporter of course brings a well-rounded education to his or her job, too.

Programs emphasizing journalism training and education are relatively recent, being almost entirely a 20th Century phenomenon. Even before about 20 years ago, many journalists received no formal training in their craft. They picked up what they could here and there. You can still do this, but most journalists don't want to settle for such an

207

uncertain way of becoming better trained for their work. In a few countries, journalists are able to go through thorough and structured apprenticeships with the media, but this isn't true in most nations. Because of the lack of resources, many Third World journalism training programs are not what reporters would like them to be (or what the sponsors would like them to be, either). Currently, the journalist who wants more training must look abroad or to outside organizations for help. There are hundreds of places throughout the world where journalism training is the main order of business. The quality of the programs is vastly uneven, and the bemused young reporter has a tough time getting much information about these programs.

Such foreign programs range from very practical, intense seminars of a few weeks' or months' duration to more traditional, academic-setting programs offering a degree in journalism or mass communication studies. Some programs are slanted towards producing journalists who will work for the government. Obviously, the short-term, intensive programs are the ones most likely to attract mid-career journalists. The four- or five-year programs more frequently suit the person just entering the field, who has fewer family and job obligations. Some of the programs carry academic degree credit and others do not.

In recent years, hundreds of Third World journalists have been offered oppportunities to study outside their countries at seminars made possible by "foreign" organizations or governments. Frequently such programs are free and the reporter is chosen to attend, either by his or her news organization or government, or by the sponsoring organization. Several nations have been especially active in offering journalistic training to Third World journalists. These include the United States, the Soviet Union, Great Britain, and some Eastern European nations. There are several well-known Latin American, African and Asian centers for journalistic training.

As you consider possibilities for foreign training, you should understand that you will be trained in a program which often reflects differing cultural, political or economic values.

Chapter 17

There is no completely "free lunch" for you. Most programs do hope to help you become a better journalist. But the sponsors of many of the programs also hope that you will come out of them at least friendly to the sponsoring organization or government. Some programs amount to an attempted indoctrination of Third World journalists so that they will absorb the political and cultural values of the sponsor.

There are several dangers in accepting training by foreign organizations or governments. If you accept free training or subsidized training from a foreign government, you can be almost assured that the sponsor hopes for at least goodwill from you as a result and a favorable outllook toward the sponsoring country. At the worst, you may find yourself segregated and brainwashed into doing things only in the manner or the policies of the sponsoring government or organization.

Of course, Third World young people have long realized that few hands are extended to them completely unselfishly. For example, they realized in many countries during past generations that even Christian mission schools exacted a price — a professed belief in Christianity. But these young people were often willing to pay that price for the only education available to them. If persons supposedly motivated only by godly love have expectations of recipients, can we be surprised at the expectations of more materialistic governments or organizations?

But realization that everything has its cost does not necessarily mean that the Third World reporter should refuse training outside his or her country. A reporter seeking training from foreign organizations or institutions should always ask how the training is to be made relevant to his or her situation at home. Such foreign training may be highly useful, but it should not be worshipped merely because its foreign. The Third World reporter should realize that some of such education may not be directly applicable to the situation in the Third World. But with these reservations, foreign training or education can frequently help. And sometimes we only appreciate our own nation or culture by having to live in a foreign one. Frequently we can learn new ideas or use new technologies which can aid us when we return to our jobs.

One of the first ways of getting information about opportunities for journalistic training is to talk to your colleagues in the media. It is very likely that some of them have received training in your own country's leading schools or have participated in training by foreign organizations or governments. They can tell you how to make contact and get more information. They can often tell you, too, how to "put your best foot forward" in making application for training, since they have successfully done so.

Other ways of finding out about journalism education include going to your nearest training school and talking to students and teachers there. They can fill you in about their own programs and often have information about other training activities as well.

Foreign embassies or consulates are other good sources to find out about training. Especially active in making such information available are France, the USSR, both Chinas, the United States, Yugoslavia, Great Britain and Canada. Some of these embassies have cultural and educational centers or libraries in which you can obtain help. Some governments directly sponsor journalistic training programs, or work with your own government on a bi-lateral basis. One unusual effort is the work of the East-West Communication Institute at the East-West Center in Honolulu, Hawaii, U.S.A. This center is mainly funded by The United States but also by Pacific area governments. Each year several dozen Pacific area journalists receive practical journalistic training at the East-West Center. This is usually done through scholarships or fellowships. The address of the East-West Center is given along with other useful addresses at the end of this chapter.

Not to be overlooked are educational and training programs of various colleges and universities throughout the world. Some of these are offered by government-run schools and others by private institutions. Most of these programs are given for academic credit and take several years' time. A few institutions, however, specialize in short-term training programs, ranging from workshops to personal tutorials. Sometimes scholarships or fellowships are available from the sponsoring institution or are made available through your own organization or government. Many fellowships include your

Chapter 17

airfare, living expenses and tuition while you are in the program. Your own ministry of information may have material about a variety of programs abroad.

WHERE TO OBTAIN INFORMATION ABOUT JOURNALISM TRAINING

This listing is not complete. The omission of any specific program should not be construed as negative. Up-to-date information is difficult to obtain, and some outstanding programs are sure to be overlooked.

Short-Term Emphasis Programs

These are usually not offered for academic credit and emphasize practical work to improve reporting or other journalistic skills.

The Institute of Culture and Communication, East-West Center, 1777 East-West Road, Honolulu, Hawaii, U.S.A. 96848. (Note: Workshops and seminars sponsored by the Culture and Communication Institute emphasize participation by persons from Asian or Pacific area countries. In a few cases, participants come from other areas.)

The Center for Foreign Journalists, 11690-A Sunrise Valley Dr., Reston, Va., 22091, U.S.A.

Centro Internacional de Estudios Superiores de Comunicacion para America Latina (CIESPAL), Almagro y Andrade Marin, Quito, Ecuador. (Note: Training programs are mainly for journalists in the Americas.)

Centre Africain de Perfectionnement des Journalistes et des Communicateurs, 9, Rue Hooker Doolittle, 1002 Tunis, Belvedere, Tunisia. (Note: This is a relatively new advanced training center connected with the Tunisian Ministry of Information. Some training programs are offered in French and Arabic and occasionally in English.)

John S. Knight Fellowships, Department of Communication, Stanford University, Stanford, California, U.S.A. 94305. (Note: Fellowships are offered for a summer program for practicing journalists. Journalists from throughout the world are eligible.)

211

Handbook for Third World Journalists

Henry W. Grady School of Journalism and Mass Communication, the University of Georgia, Athens, Georgia, U.S.A. 30602. (Note: Both short-term, non-credit, individual tutorials and training programs are offered to foreign journalists as well as regular master's degree and undergraduate work. Contact Dr. Al Hester.) No scholarships are available for these programs. Contracts are worked out with individuals or their institutions or agencies.

International Journalists' Training Course, Thomson Foundation Editorial Study Centre, Cardiff, Wales, England.

Transnational Communications Center, the Media Institute, 3017 M Street N.W., Washington, D.C. 20007 (Note: Conducts education programs for foreign journalists and communication specialists.)

International Organization of Journalists, Parizska 9, 110 01 Prague 1, Czechoslovakia. (Note: Sponsors a number of training programs and is also a source of information about training programs in Eastern European countries.)

The Indian Institute of Mass Communication, D-13 South Extension Part II, New Delhi, India.

Long-Term Emphasis Programs

Many of these programs carry academic credit and last for a year or more. Sometimes scholarships are available. Some of these schools may also offer shorter-term programs.

School of Journalism, University of Missouri, Columbia, Missouri, U.S.A. 65205. Undergraduate and graduate work.

School of Journalism and Mass Communication, University of Wisconsin, Madison, U.S.A. 53706. Undergraduate and graduate work.

School of Communication, University of Washington, Seattle, Washington, U.S.A. 98195. Undergraduate and graduate work.

Department of Journalism, University of Texas at Austin, Austin, Texas, U.S.A. 78712. Undergraduate and graduate work.

School of Journalism and Mass Communication, University of Minnesota, Minneapolis, Minnesota, 55455. Graduate and undergraduate work.

Chapter 17

Graduate School of Journalism, Columbia University, New York, New York, U.S.A. 10027. Gradauate work only.

The American University, Journalism Department, Cairo, Egypt.

Institute of Communication, Cairo University, Cairo, Egypt.

Kenya Institute of Mass Communication, Ministry of Information and Broadcasting, P.O. Box 42422, Nairobi, Kenya.

Hong Kong Baptist College, Department of Communication, 224 Waterloo Road, Kowloon, Hong Kong.

Osmania University, Department of Journalism, Osmania University Campus, Hyderabad 500007, India.

Sophia University, Faculty of Letters, Department of Communication, 7 Kioicho, Chiyoda-ku, Tokyo, Japan.

Australian Association for Tertiary Education in Journalism, Mitchell College of Advanced Education, Bathurst, New South Wales, Australia. (Note: Can furnish information on individual schools offering journalism programs.)

The Journalism Faculty, Moscow University, Prospekt Marxa 20, Moscow, USSR.

Department of Mass Communications, University of Salzburg, Sigmund Haffner Gasse 183, A-5020 Salzburg, Austria.

Latin American Institute for Transnational Studies, Apartado 85-025, Mexico 20, D.F., Mexico. (Advanced Training).

Handbook for Third World Journalists

Appendix I
How to Find News

Some young reporters want to know how to find stories. Here are some tips from reporters with many years of experience.

1. Have a curiosity. If you don't have curiosity, you will never make a good reporter. If you don't always wonder WHY, then there's no hope for you. Even elegant writing style plays second fiddle to wanting to know the why-of-things.

2. Get out of the office. Stories do not lurk behind the water-cooler in the office. You get very few reading the paper or working a cross-word puzzle. And if you stay in the office, the sub-editor will call upon you when there are things to do. Out of sight, out of mind. If you must stay in the office, hide behind a post — but that won't help you get stories.

3. Don't ask your sources, "What's New?" Nothing is new to most of them, since their jobs are routine. They wouldn't know a good news story if it hit them over the head (most of them anyway.) You are the trained news-hunter.

4. Talk to a great variety of people. Listen to what you hear in coffee houses or pubs.

5. Read specialized periodicals in your field of reporting, if they are available. Subscribe to one or two if you can afford to. If you write about local government, for example, there are probably publications about it, which the local governmental officials read.

6. Go to diplomatic parties and receptions. You can learn a lot here, as well as get some free food and something to drink.

7. Read your own newspaper. Lots of reporters don't like to read anything written by anyone else. Don't be lazy. Keep up with events in your paper. Every reporter has an obligation to read his or her own paper, and several others if possible.

8. Don't hesitate to steal ideas from other countries' newspapers, or papers other than your own. There is no copyright on ideas, only on the precise way of expressing them. You can frequently localize a story which has application to your area.

9. Read official communiques, as dull as they often are. They may contain the germ of a story.

10. Watch television and listen to the radio. The other media have been known to do a good story once in a while which you can adapt.

11. Monitor foreign news broadcasts and programs on shortwave. These will often educate you and broaden your perspective.

12. Keep a future file. This will tickle your memory and stimulate you to thinking about stories which need covering. The editor will value you as an organized reporter if you keep a file on what is coming up.

13. Consistently keep contact with your sources. The more often you see them, the more likely they are to trust you (unless you are an untrustworthy person, in which case the more they see you, the more they will mistrust you.)

14. Check foreign embassy offices frequently, especially press officers. Try to talk directly to them.

15. Don't ignore businessmen. They frequently must know what is going on, if they are to survive.

16. People who work at airports and harbors are frequent-y knowledgeable about comings-and-goings of interesting people. Have a source who knows about departures and arrivals. Be friendly with airlines and shipping companies.

17. Spend time in the market or bazaar. This is necessary to have the feel of situations. You won't get it by talking to bureaucrats or by staying in the press club.

18. Know several languages, if your country is multilingual. Then you won't have to get information second-hand.

19. Talk with fellow journalists. This can be incestuous, but you will occasionally get a good idea for a story.

20. Occasionally university professors and administrators are news sources. Know a few of them and check them to see what is going on.

Appendix I

21. Realize that you will not get stories every time you check with sources. Some time is wisely invested in finding out what their interests are and what makes them tick. This will help you get stories later.

22. Swap gossip with politicians and officials. Most love to hear what others say about them, and will also give you tidbits of information.

23. Take time to walk around your city or area. Look with fresh eyes at what is happening. Driving a car will not do this as well. Experience your community — don't isolate yourself.

24. Once in a while, go off in a cave somewhere and THINK. Take a paper pad with you and write down some possible story ideas. This is not time spent day-dreaming. It will pay off in better ideas.

25. Remember editors love a self-starting reporter with ideas. They have trouble getting ideas themselves, and they will embrace you if you make their lives easier.

News Sleuth at Work.

Appendix II
List of Helpful Readings

NOTE: The following readings have been selected with any eye to what might be of help to practicing journalists. These books should help you to improve your skills and understanding of journalism and mass communications. All were in print at the time of compilation. Prices are not included, since these are subject to frequent change.

Agee, Warren, Philip H. Ault and Edwin Emery, *Introduction to Mass Communications* (Silver Anniversary ed.) (New York: Harper and Row, 1985). The oldest and one of the best books to give you an overview on the whole field. Available in English, French, Spanish and Portuguese.

Callihan, E.L., *Grammar for Journalists* (Philadelphia, Pa., U.S.A.: Chilton, 1980). An excellent overview of English grammar for those who need extra help.

Dominick, Joseph R., and Roger D. Wimmer, *Mass Media Research* (Belmont, Calif., U.S.A.: Wadsworth, Inc., 1983). A good review on how to use research in the mass media. Handy for journalists who need to know more in this area.

Izard, Ralph S., Hugh M. Culbertson and Donald A. Lambert, *Fundamentals of News Reporting*, (4th ed.) (Dubuque, Iowa, U.S.A.: Kendall-Hunt, 1983). One of the most practical and easy to understand of the American reporting texts.

Jendoiubi, Mehdi, *Journalisme de'Agence: Journalisme de Base* (Tunis, Tunisia: Institut de Presse et des Sciences de l'Information, 1984). An excellent book on news agency reporting and Editing. In French.

Kivikuru, Ullamaija, and Tapio Varis, eds., *Approaches to International Communication* (Helsinki, Finnish National Commission for UNESCO, 1986).

219

Metzler, Ken, *Creative Interviewing* (Englewood Cliffs, N.J., U.S.A.: Prentice-Hall, 1977). The best book on interviewing techniques available. Easy to understand and use.

Nelson, Roy Paul, *Articles and Features* (Boston, Mass., U.S.A.: Houghton-Mifflin, 1978). A good book on magazine and feature writing, but emphasizing free-lance in U.S. applications.

Reintjes, J. Francis, *Copy-Processing Systems for Small Newspapers* (Cambridge, Mass., U.S.A.: Massachusetts Institute of Technology, 1979).

Rivadeneira Prada, Raul, *Periodismo* (Mexico City, Mex.: Editorial Trillas, 1977). Gives both practical and theoretical understanding of journalism. In Spanish.

Rivers, William L., *Magazine Editing in the '80s* (Belmont, Calif.,U.S.A.: Wadsworth Publishing, 1983). One of the best in its field.

Rosen, Marvin J., *Introduction to Photography*: a Self-Directing Approach (Boston: Houghton-Mifflin, 1976). An excellent, practical guide to being a photographer.

White, Ted, et al., *Broadcast News Writing, Reporting, and Production* (New York: Macmillan, 1984).